quick & easy
sauces

over 70 delicious recipes to transform
everyday dishes and desserts

Contributing Editor
Christine France

HERMES
HOUSE

This edition is published by Hermes House

Hermes House is an imprint of Anness Publishing Ltd
Hermes House, 88–89 Blackfriars Road, London SE1 8HA
tel. 020 7401 2077; fax 020 7633 9499
info@anness.com

© Anness Publishing Ltd 2005

A CIP catalogue record for this book is available from the British Library.

Publisher: Joanna Lorenz
Editorial Director: Helen Sudell
Editors: Simona Hill and Elizabeth Woodland
Photography by: Karl Adamson, Edward Allwright, David Armstrong,
Steve Baxter, James Duncan, John Freeman, Michelle Garrett, John Heseltine,
Amanda Heywood, Janine Hosegood, Don Last, William Lingwood,
Patrick McLeavy, Michael Michaels, Thomas Odulate, Debbie Patterson
and Juliet Piddington.
Recipes by: Alex Barker, Angela Boggiano, Carla Capalbo,
Jacqueline Clark, Carole Clements, Roz Denny, Nicola Diggins,
Tessa Evelegh, Joanna Farrow, Christine France, Silvana Franco,
Shirley Gill, Nicola Graimes, Juliet Harbutt, Christine Ingram,
Peter Jordan, Soheila Kimberley, Ruby Le Bois, Lesley Macklay,
Sue Maggs, Maggie Mayhew, Sallie Morris, Janice Murfitt, Maggie Pannell,
Louise Pickford, Katherine Richmond, Laura Washburn,
Steven Wheeler, Kate Whiteman and Jeni Wright.
Designer: Simon Wilder
Cover Designed by: Whitelight Design
Production Controller: Wendy Lawson

Previously published as part of a larger volume, *Cook's Book of Sauces*.

1 3 5 7 9 10 8 6 4 2

NOTES

Bracketed terms are intended for American readers.

For all recipes, quantities are given in both metric and imperial
measures and, where appropriate, measures are also given in standard cups and spoons.
Follow one set, but not a mixture because they are not interchangeable.

Standard spoon and cup measures are level.
1 tsp = 5ml, 1 tbsp = 15ml, 1 cup = 250ml/8fl oz

Australian standard tablespoons are 20ml.
Australian readers should use 3 tsp in place of 1 tbsp
for measuring small quantities of salt etc.

Medium (US large) eggs are used unless otherwise stated.

Contents

Introduction

Exactly the right sauce, properly prepared, is what turns good food into a great dish. Famous chefs, from Antonin Carême in the 19th century to today's flamboyant television stars, all recognize the importance of a perfect sauce, from a delicious Italian pesto to a rich tomato, a tangy orange or a divine chocolate sauce.

This book is packed with recipes for every kind of sweet and savoury sauce, as well as helpful suggestions for serving them. It begins with a foundation of favourite classics, including the basic repertoire of many cuisines from around the world. Pasta sauces, deservedly, have a whole chapter devoted to them. Recipes range from simple and refreshing vegetable sauces to rich and creamy classics and also include some exciting and innovative ideas for livening up whatever you have in your pantry.

There is more to meat and poultry than traditional gravy, and Sauces for Meat Dishes offers a fabulous choice of fresh and fruity, hot and spicy, and sweet and sour accompaniments. Sauces for Fish Dishes contains delicate and subtly flavoured sauces to complement white fish and rich, robust and lively sauces for those with a sophisticated palate. Sauces for Vegetarian

Above: Grilled skewered chicken served with this tasty satay sauce is always a favourite at parties.

Below: The juices from the cooked lamb sausages adds a rich flavour to the tomato sauce.

Below: For a quick and tasty dish, stir-fry squid with a spicy black bean sauce.

Dishes range from substantial cheese-based accompaniments to light and airy sauces that demonstrate just how versatile vegetables can be. Finally, Sauces for Sweet Dishes provides a wealth of wonderful and astonishingly quick and simple ways to brighten up basics, such as ice cream, meringues and fresh fruit.

Whether you are a novice cook who wants to add interest and new flavours to weekday meals, or an expert who would like to broaden your culinary repertoire, understanding the basics of sauce-making will provide a firm foundation for a lifetime of creative cooking. Many sauce-making ingredients such as flour and fat are found in every kitchen. Just adding a few other well-chosen ingredients will provide you with a pantry from which to make a whole range of interesting and flavourful accompaniments to meals.

Sauce-making doesn't require any specialist equipment, and much of what you already own will be sufficient, such as a selection of pans, bowls, whisks, ladles, sieves, weighing scales and measuring jugs or cups.

The following pages include all the basic methods of sauce-making, from a good home-made stock, to savoury egg sauces and dessert sauces, and there are plenty of hints and tips to help you produce the best results.

Below: Try a sweet dipping sauce to transform fruit into a simple and irresistible dessert.

Left: Make a sweet dish look extra special by drizzling a delicious fruity dessert sauce to decorate the plate.

Below left: By using a food processor you can make a smooth and creamy mayonnaise in just a few seconds.

Below: A sauce of fresh vegetables tossed with cooked pasta is ideal for a quick and tasty, light lunch, supper or dinner.

Making Basic Stocks

A good home-made stock is simple to make and adds a rich flavour to all kinds of savoury sauces. Commercial stock (bouillon) cubes and bouillon powder won't match the flavour of home-made stock. However, they can be very useful for enriching a stock that lacks flavour: heat it until boiling then stir in a stock cube or a teaspoon of bouillon powder until dissolved. Each recipe below makes approximately 1 litre/1¾ pints/4 cups.

Beef Stock

INGREDIENTS

675g/1½lb shin of beef, diced
1 large onion, chopped
1 large carrot, chopped
1 celery stick, chopped
bouquet garni
6 black peppercorns
2.5ml/½ tsp sea salt
1.75 litres/3 pints/7½ cups water

1 Place all the ingredients in a large pan and gradually bring to the boil.

2 Cover the pan and simmer very gently for 4 hours, skimming occasionally to remove scum. Strain the stock and cool.

Fish Stock

INGREDIENTS

1kg/2¼lb white fish bones and trimmings
1 large onion, sliced
1 large carrot, sliced
1 celery stick, sliced
bouquet garni
6 white peppercorns
2.5ml/½ tsp sea salt
150ml/¼ pint/⅔ cup dry white wine
1 litre/1¾ pints/4 cups water

1 Place the ingredients in a pan and bring to the boil.

2 Skim any scum from the surface, cover the pan and simmer for 20 minutes. Strain and cool.

Chicken Stock

INGREDIENTS

1 chicken carcass
chicken giblets
1 leek, chopped
1 celery stick, chopped
bouquet garni
5ml/1 tsp white peppercorns
2.5ml/½ tsp sea salt
1.75 litres/3 pints/7½ cups water

1 Break up the carcass, place in a pan with the remaining ingredients. Bring to the boil.

2 Reduce the heat, cover and simmer gently for about 2½ hours, skimming to remove scum. Strain the stock and cool.

Vegetable Stock

INGREDIENTS

500g/1¼lb chopped mixed vegetables, e.g. onions, carrots, celery, leeks
bouquet garni
6 black peppercorns
2.5ml/½ tsp sea salt
1 litre/1¾ pints/4 cups water

1 Place all the ingredients in a large pan and slowly bring to the boil.

2 Skim any scum from the surface, then cover the pan and simmer gently for 30 minutes. Strain the stock and allow to cool.

Making a Bouquet Garni

A traditional bouquet garni usually contains a bay leaf, a sprig of thyme and a few sprigs of parsley, but this can be varied according to taste, and to suit the dish you are making. Other vegetables or herbs you may like to include are a piece of celery stick for poultry dishes; a rosemary sprig for beef or lamb; or a piece of fennel or leek, or a strip of lemon rind, to flavour fish dishes.

Tie the herbs together firmly with fine cotton string, so the bundle is easy to remove from the stock after cooking.

Or, tie the herbs in a square of muslin (cheesecloth). Leave a long length of the string to tie to the pan handle.

Keeping Stock Clear

For a clear soup it is important to keep the stock clear; avoid boiling the soup, and skim the top from time to time.

1 Trim any fat from the meat or bones before adding to the stock pan, as this can create a cloudy stock.

2 Keep the heat at a low simmer, and skim off any scum as it gathers on the surface during cooking. Most vegetables can be added to stock for flavour, but potatoes tend to break down and make the stock cloudy so it's best to avoid these.

3 Strain the cooked stock through a sieve lined with muslin (cheese-cloth), and avoid pressing the solids, as this may spoil the stock's clarity.

Removing Fat from Stock

Excess fat should always be removed from the liquid to improve the look and taste of the stock; it also helps keep the stock clear.

1 Let the stock stand until the fat settles on the surface, then skim off as much fat as possible with a large, shallow spoon. To absorb even more grease, blot the surface of the stock with several layers of kitchen paper.

2 Then, drop in a few ice cubes. The fat will set around the ice so it can be simply spooned off.

3 Alternatively, allow the stock to cool on a work surface, then chill in the refrigerator until the fat layer rises to the surface and sets. Then the fat can simply be lifted off. Use a large spoon to remove the solidified fat and discard it.

How to Store Stock

Stock will keep for up to a week in the refrigerator, and freezes well. Reduce it first so that it takes up less room in the freezer.

1 To freeze, pour into airtight containers, allowing 2.5cm/1in headspace for expansion, then seal and freeze for up to 3 months.

2 To freeze stock in convenient portions to add to sauces, pour into ice cube trays for freezing.

COOK'S TIP

• Use salt sparingly at the beginning of cooking – if you are going to reduce the stock it will become much more salty.

• To make a brown stock from beef or veal bones, roast the bones in a hot oven for 40 minutes. Add the vegetables half-way through the roasting time. Deglaze the pan with a little water and simmer the bones and vegetables as usual.

• To make a stock with a concentrated flavour, simmer the stock until reduced by half. Continue to reduce the stock until it will coat the back of a spoon. At its most concentrated it will set as a solid jelly and give you a quick and easy way to add rich flavour to sauces and soups.

Flour-based Sauces

The standard way to adjust the consistency of a sauce is to thicken it with one of the different availa' ,pes of flour. There are three basic methods for this – roux, blending or all-in-one. Once you've learned the basic skills of these methods, you'll be able to tackle any flour-thickened sauce without problems.

Many of the classic white sauces are based on a "roux", which is simply a cooked mixture of flour and fat. The most basic white sauce uses milk, but by varying the liquid used other well-known white sauces can be made. For a classic béchamel sauce, the milk is flavoured first by infusing (steeping) with pieces of vegetables and herbs. For velouté sauce, the milk is replaced with stock, giving the sauce a more opaque appearance, and the thickened sauce may be enriched with cream after cooking. Brown sauces or gravy are made by browning the roux, usually with onions, before adding stock or other liquid such as wine.

Basic Recipe for White Roux Sauces

Using the classic roux method, you can adjust the amount of thickening to create varying consistencies of sauces. A pouring sauce is used, as it suggests, to be poured directly over foods when serving. The slightly thicker coating sauce is used to make a smooth covering for fish or vegetables.

For a pouring consistency:
15g/¹/₂ oz/1 tbsp butter
15g/¹/₂ oz/2 tbsp flour
300ml/¹/₂ pint/1¹/₄ cups liquid

For a coating consistency:
25g/1oz/2 tbsp butter
25g/1oz/¹/₄ cup flour
300 ml/¹/₂ pint/1¹/₄ cups liquid

Making a Roux-based White Sauce

The trick to making a roux is to stir the pan over the whole of the base, and add the liquid gradually; it is a good idea to heat the milk or stock before adding to the roux as this helps avoid lumps.

Melt the butter in a pan, then add the flour. To prevent browning, cook on a low heat and stir with a wooden spoon, for 1–2 minutes. Allow the mixture to bubble until it resembles a honeycomb in texture. It is important to cook well at this point, to allow the starch grains in the flour to swell and burst, and avoid lumps forming later.

2 Remove the pan from the heat and gradually stir in the liquid, which may be either hot or cold. Return to the heat and stir until boiling and thickened. Reduce the heat and simmer, stirring constantly, for 2 minutes, until the sauce is thickened and smooth.

Blending Method

Sauces which are thickened by the blending method are usually made with cornflour (cornstarch), arrowroot, potato flour or sauce flour. Cornflour and sauce flour make light, glossy, lump-free sauces, which are good for freezing as the starch does not break down. If you need a crystal-clear result for glazing, use arrowroot or potato flour. The liquid may be milk, stock, fruit juice, or syrup from canned or poached fruit. As a guide, you will need 20g/³/₄ oz/3 tbsp cornflour or sauce flour to thicken 300ml/¹/₂ pint/1¹/₄ cups liquid to a pouring consistency. Arrowroot or potato flour are slightly stronger, so use approximately 15g/¹/₂ oz to 300ml/¹/₂ pint/1¹/₄ cups liquid to obtain the same consistency.

Place the flour in a bowl and add just enough liquid to make a smooth, thin paste. Heat the remaining liquid in a pan until almost boiling.

2 Pour a little of the liquid on to the blended mixture, stirring. Pour the blended mixture back into the pan, whisking constantly to avoid lumps. Return to the heat and stir until boiling, then simmer gently for 2 minutes, stirring until thickened and smooth.

All-in-one Method

This method uses the same ingredients and proportions as the roux method, but the liquid added must be cold.

Place the flour, butter and cold liquid in the pan and whisk with a sauce whisk or balloon whisk over a moderate heat until boiling. Stir over the heat for 2 minutes, until thickened and smooth.

Using an Egg Yolk Liaison

This is a simple way to lightly thicken hot milk or stock, cream or reduced poaching liquids, and is good for enriching savoury white or velouté sauces. Two egg yolks should be enough to enrich and thicken about 300ml/½ pint/1¼ cups liquid, depending on the recipe. A mixture of egg yolk and cream has the same effect, but add it when the pan is off the heat to avoid curdling.

Place two egg yolks in a small bowl and stir in 30ml/2 tbsp of the hot liquid or sauce. Stir the egg mixture into the remaining liquid or sauce and heat gently, stirring, without boiling.

Making Beurre Manié

Literally translated as "kneaded butter", this is a mixture of flour and butter, which can be stirred into a hot sauce, poaching liquid or cooked dish such as a casserole or ragoût to thicken the juices. It's a convenient way to adjust the consistency of a sauce or dish at the end of cooking, and is easy to control as you can add the exact amount required, adjusting as it thickens. The butter adds flavour and a glossy sheen to the finished sauce. Any leftover beurre manié can be stored in a covered jar in the refrigerator for about 2 weeks, ready to use in sauces, soups, stews or casseroles.

1 Place equal amounts of butter and flour in a bowl and knead together with your fingers or a wooden spoon to make a smooth paste.

2 Drop teaspoonfuls of the beurre manié paste into the simmering sauce, whisking thoroughly to incorporate each spoonful before adding the next, until the sauce is thickened and smooth and the desired consistency is achieved.

Infusing Flavours

To infuse (steep) flavours into milk, stock or other liquids before using in sauces such as béchamel, pour the liquid into a pan and add thin slices or dice of onion, carrot and celery, a bouquet garni, peppercorns or a mace blade. Bring the liquid slowly to the boil, then remove the pan from the heat. Cover and leave to stand for about 10 minutes. Strain the milk to remove the flavourings before use.

Adding Flavourings to Flour-based Sauces

Once you've made your basic sauce, try some of these quick flavour additions to pep up the flavour and add variety:
• Stir 50g/2oz/½ cup grated Cheddar or other strong cheese into a basic white sauce with 5ml/1 tsp wholegrain mustard and a generous dash of Worcestershire sauce.
• Wine livens up the flavour of most stock-based sauces – boil 60ml/4 tbsp red or white wine in a pan until well-reduced, then stir into the finished sauce with a grating of nutmeg or black pepper.
• Parsley, or any fresh herbs will infuse and change the flavour of a white sauce. Add chopped herbs a few minutes before the end of the cooking time.

Correcting a Lumpy Sauce

If your flour-thickened sauce has gone lumpy, don't despair – it can be corrected.

1 First, try whisking the sauce hard with a light wire whisk in the pan to smooth out the lumps, then reheat gently, stirring.

2 If the sauce is still not smooth, rub it through a fine sieve, pressing firmly with a wooden spoon. Return to the pan and reheat gently, stirring.

3 Alternatively, pour the sauce into a food processor and process until smooth. Return to the pan and reheat gently, stirring.

Keeping Sauces Hot

1 To keep sauces hot, pour into a heatproof bowl and place over a pan of very gently simmering water.

2 To prevent a skin from forming over the surface, place a sheet of lightly oiled or wetted greaseproof (waxed) paper or baking parchment directly on to the surface of the sauce. Stir before serving.

Degreasing Sauces

Even after skimming any surplus fat from a finished hot sauce or gravy with a flat metal spoon, final traces of fat may still remain. These can be removed by dragging the flat surface of a piece of kitchen paper over the surface to absorb traces of grease.

Making a Roux-based Brown Sauce

A brown roux is the basis of many meat dish sauces. Onions or other vegetables are usually browned in fat before flour is added. The fat can be a mixture of butter and oil, or dripping. Butter alone is unsuitable as it burns easily at high temperatures. Use about 30ml/2 tbsp oil and about 25g/1oz/¼ cup flour for the roux to about 600ml/1 pint/2½ cups reduced brown stock. At the last moment, stir in 15g/½oz/1 tbsp chilled butter to give a glossy finish.

1 Melt the fat and fry one small, finely chopped onion until softened and golden. Sprinkle on the flour and stir in with a wooden spoon. Stir over a low heat for 4–5 minutes, until the mixture colours to a rich brown.

2 Remove the pan from the heat and gradually stir in the liquid, which may be either hot or cold. Return to the heat and stir until boiling. Simmer gently, stirring, for a further 2 minutes, until the sauce is thick and smooth. The sauce may be strained to remove the onions at this stage.

Using a Deglazed Sauce

Deglazing means adding a small amount of liquid to the pan after roasting or pan-frying to dilute the rich concentrated juices into a simple sauce. Spoon off the excess fat, and then scrape up the sediment from the pan bottom with a spoon as you stir in the liquid.

1 Tilt the pan and spoon off excess fat from the surface of the juices.

2 Stir in a few tablespoons of wine, stock or cream.

3 Simmer over a moderate heat, stirring and scraping up the sediment as the sauce boils. Boil rapidly to reduce the juices until syrupy, then pour over the food.

Making Traditional Gravy

Good gravy should be smooth and glossy, never heavy and floury. Generally speaking, it's best to use the minimum of thickening, but this can be adjusted to your own taste. Providing the meat has been roasted to a rich brown, the meat juices will have enough colour to colour the gravy. If it is too pale, a few drops of gravy browning can be stirred in to darken it slightly.

1 To make a thickened gravy, skim off all except about 15ml/1 tbsp of the fat from the juices in the roasting pan after roasting meat. Gradually stir in about 15ml/1 tbsp flour, scraping up the sediment and meat juices.

2 Place the tin directly over the heat and stir until bubbling. Cook, stirring for 1–2 minutes until the roux is brown and the flour cooked.

3 Gradually stir in the liquid, which may be either stock or vegetable water, until the gravy is of the thickness desired. Simmer for 2–3 minutes, stirring constantly, and adjust the seasoning to taste.

Ideas for Deglazed Sauces

Brandy and Peppercorn – deglaze the pan with brandy or sherry, stir in cream and coarsely ground black pepper. Serve with grilled (broiled) or fried steaks.

Red Wine and Cranberry – deglaze the pan with red wine and stir in cranberry sauce or jelly. This recipe is good with roast game or turkey.

Sauce Bercy – deglaze with dry white wine or vermouth, stir in a finely chopped shallot and sauté gently until soft. Add cream, lemon juice and chopped parsley. Excellent with fried or poached fish.

Adding Flavourings to a Brown Sauce

A well-flavoured brown stock, which has been reduced by between one-third to a half, is the basis of a good brown sauce but it can also be enhanced by the addition of a variety of flavourings.

• A handful of chopped fresh basil, chives or flat leaf parsley, stirred into the sauce just before serving, will improve the flavour and look of a basic brown sauce.

• For game or poultry, stir a little curry paste, two crushed cloves of garlic and one finely chopped onion into the roux and cook for about 5 minutes before adding the stock. Stir in a handful of chopped fresh coriander (cilantro) just before serving.

• Add coarsely grated orange rind to a basic brown sauce and serve it with duck or game.

Vegetable Sauces and Salsas

Many sauces use vegetables for flavour, colour and texture, and there's no end to the healthy variations you can make with a few very simple techniques. Puréed or chopped vegetables can be used to make both cooked sauces and fresh salsas. Vegetable sauces and salsas make fresh, colourful, low-fat alternatives to more conventional sauces, and they are invariably very easy and quick to make.

Basic Tomato Sauce

For the best flavour, use plum tomatoes. If using canned make sure they are not already flavoured with herbs. Peel fresh tomatoes before using. Fresh tomatoes rather than canned tomatoes can be used. Substitute about 500g/1¼lb of tomatoes for each 400g/14oz can.

Makes about 450ml/¾ pint/ scant 2 cups

INGREDIENTS

15ml/1 tbsp olive oil
15g/½oz/1 tbsp butter
1 garlic clove, finely chopped
1 small onion, finely chopped
1 celery stick, finely chopped
400g/14oz can chopped tomatoes
handful of basil leaves
salt and ground black pepper

⎮ Heat the olive oil and butter in a heavy pan.

2 When the oil starts to bubble, add the garlic, onion and celery. Sauté the ingredients gently over a low heat, stirring occasionally, for 15–20 minutes or until the onions soften and are just beginning to colour.

3 Stir the chopped tomatoes into the sauce and bring to the boil. Cover and simmer gently for 10–15 minutes, stirring occasionally, until thick.

4 Tear or roughly chop the basil leaves and stir into the sauce. Adjust the seasoning with salt and pepper and serve hot.

COOK'S TIP

A soffritto (Italian), or sofrito (Spanish), is the basis of many Mediterranean meat or tomato sauces. It's such a classic that some recipes list "soffritto" simply as an ingredient with no other explanation. A basic soffritto usually consists of onion, garlic, green (bell) pepper and celery, sometimes with a little carrot or pancetta. The finely chopped ingredients are sautéed slowly to soften and caramelize the flavours and are used in soups and sauces.

Making Quick Salsa Crudo

This is literally a "raw sauce" of vegetables or fruits, and it's easy to create your own combinations of flavour. A good basic start for a salsa crudo is chillies, (bell) peppers, onions, and garlic. Serve with grilled (broiled) chicken, pork, lamb or fish.

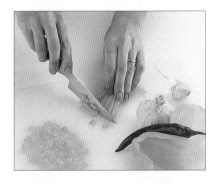

⎮ Peel, seed or trim the vegetables as necessary, then use a sharp knife to cut into small, even dice. Try to combine texture and colour as well as taste, and use chillies and other very spicy ingredients sparingly. Put all the diced ingredients into a bowl.

2 Add 15–30ml/1–2 tbsp olive oil and a squeeze of lime or lemon juice and stir in finely chopped fresh basil, coriander (cilantro), flat leaf parsley or mint, to enrich the flavour. Season to taste and toss well before serving.

To Peel Tomatoes

1 Cut a small cross in the skins of the tomatoes. Bring a pan of water to the boil and add the tomatoes. Turn off the heat and leave for 30 seconds, then lift out carefully with a slotted spoon and place in a bowl of cold water. Using a small knife, peel off the skins.

2 Alternatively, place the tomato firmly on the prongs of a fork and hold in a gas flame until the skin blisters and splits. When the tomatoes are cool enough to handle, peel off the skins using a small knife.

Chargrilling Vegetables for Purées and Sauces

Many puréed sauces or salsas call for cooked or chargrilled vegetables. Chargrilling on a barbecue is the best way to get the finest flavour from many vegetables, such as (bell) peppers, aubergines (eggplants), tomatoes, garlic or onions, tenderizing the flesh and retaining and caramelizing the flavourful juices. Since this method is not always practical, the next best is to roast the vegetables under a grill (broiler).

Roasted Vegetable Sauce

Serve roasted vegetable sauce with pork, ham, poultry or game. If you prefer a sauce with more texture, simply process for a shorter time.

Makes about 300ml/¹/₂ pint/1¹/₄ cups

INGREDIENTS

2 red or orange (bell) peppers
1 small onion
1 small aubergine (eggplant)
2 tomatoes with skins removed
2 garlic cloves, unpeeled
30–45ml/2–3 tbsp olive oil
15ml/1 tbsp lemon juice
25g/1oz/¹/₂ cup fresh white breadcrumbs

1 Cut the peppers, onion and aubergine in half, leaving the skins on, and, if necessary, remove any seeds and core. Place the vegetables cut-side down on a baking sheet with the garlic cloves. Place under a very hot grill (broiler) or in a hot oven until the skins are blackened and charred, and the flesh is tender.

2 Remove from the heat and leave until cool enough to handle, then peel off the skins from the peppers and onions.

3 Scoop the flesh from the aubergines, and squeeze the flesh from the garlic.

4 Place all the vegetables in a blender or food processor and process to a very smooth purée, adding oil and lemon juice to taste. If you prefer a very smooth sauce, rub the purée through a fine sieve.

5 To thicken a vegetable purée, stir in a handful of fresh breadcrumbs and process for a few seconds to the desired consistency.

Savoury Butter Sauces

The simplest sauce of all is a melted butter sauce, flavoured with lemon juice or herbs – ideal to drizzle over a simply cooked piece of fish or vegetables. A more refined version of this is clarified butter sauce, which is butter with the moisture and impurities removed. Emulsions of butter with vinegar or other flavourings make deliciously rich beurre blanc or hollandaise sauce. Cold, flavoured butters are useful to add last-minute melting flavours on to hot foods, and can be shaped prettily for extra garnish.

Blender Hollandaise

Hollandaise is a wonderfully rich butter sauce, rather like a hot mayonnaise. This quick method eliminates whisking by hand and uses a blender to incorporate the ingredients to a thick, smooth emulsion where two liquids are combined by the dispersion of one in the other.

Makes 250ml/8fl oz/1 cup

INGREDIENTS

60ml/4 tbsp white wine vinegar
6 peppercorns
1 bay leaf
3 egg yolks
175g/6oz/¾ cup clarified butter
salt and ground black pepper

Place the wine vinegar, peppercorns and bay leaf in a small pan and heat until boiling, then simmer to reduce to about 15ml/1 tbsp. Remove from the heat and discard the flavourings.

2 Place the egg yolks in the blender goblet and start the motor. Add the reduced white wine vinegar liquid through the feeder tube and blend for 10 seconds.

3 Heat the butter until hot. With the motor running, pour the butter through the feeder tube in a thin, steady stream until thick and smooth. Adjust the seasoning to taste with salt and pepper, and serve warm with poached fish, eggs or vegetables.

PREVENTING CURDLING

If hollandaise sauce is overheated, or if the butter is added too quickly, it may curdle and become slightly granular in texture. If this happens, remove it from the heat immediately, before the sauce separates.

Quickly drop an ice cube into the sauce, then beat hard until the cube melts and cools the sauce. It also helps to stand the base of the pan in a bowl of iced water while whisking in the ice cube.

Beurre Blanc

This is one of the simplest sauces to make. White wine and white wine vinegar are reduced over a high heat to produce an intense flavour. Butter is whisked into the liquid to enrich and thicken it. It is good with grilled (broiled) or poached fish or chicken.

Place 45ml/3 tbsp each of white wine vinegar and dry white wine in a small pan with a finely chopped shallot. Bring to the boil and boil until reduced to about 15ml/1 tbsp.

2 Cut 225g/8oz/1 cup chilled unsalted (sweet) butter into small cubes. On a low heat, gradually whisk in the butter, piece by piece, allowing each piece to melt and be absorbed before adding the next. Season to taste and serve immediately.

How to Clarify Butter

Ideal for serving with vegetables such as asparagus or artichokes, clarified butter is butter which has been melted and has had all the salts, moisture and impurities removed, leaving it clear, with a rich, pure flavour. Clarified butter, called ghee in Indian cooking, keeps longer and can be heated to higher temperatures than ordinary butter without the risk of burning. It can be used for sautéing, and in sauces it gives a mild flavour and a high gloss. There are two main methods of clarifying:

Place the butter in a pan with an equal quantity of water. Heat until the butter melts. Remove the pan from the heat and leave to cool until the butter sets. Carefully lift out the fat, leaving the water and solids behind.

Alternatively, melt the butter in a small pan over a very low heat, then skim off the froth with a slotted spoon. Pour the rest through a sieve lined with fine muslin (cheesecloth), to strain out the solids.

Making Savoury Butters

Flavoured butters can be shaped or piped decoratively to serve with steaks or poached or grilled (broiled) fish.

To make a herb-flavoured butter, finely chop your choice of fresh herbs. Beat the butter until softened then stir in the herbs to mix evenly.

Making Shaped Slices

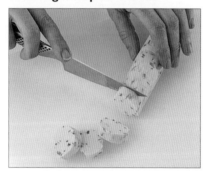

To make butter slices, chill the softened herb butter lightly. With your hands, roll the butter into a long sausage-shape and wrap in baking parchment or clear film (plastic wrap). Chill and cut off slices of the butter as required.

Piping Butter

Using a star nozzle, pipe softened butter on to baking parchment.

Making Shaped Butters

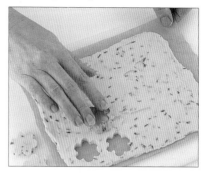

To make shaped butter pats, chill lightly, roll out the butter between two sheets of baking parchment. Chill until firm, then remove the top sheet and stamp out small shapes with a cutter.

Flavourings for Savoury Butters

As well as being the traditional accompaniment to steaks, flavoured butters can be rubbed on to meat before roasting or spread over chops before grilling (broiling) or cooking on a barbecue. They can also be spread on fish that is foil-wrapped and baked or used as you would garlic butter to make deliciously flavoured breads.

• Finely chopped herbs, e.g. chives, parsley, dill, mint, thyme or rosemary. Use one herb or a combination of your choice and add as much as the butter will comfortably absorb, or to achieve the desired flavour.
• Finely grated lemon, lime or orange rind and juice.
• Finely chopped canned anchovy fillets.
• Finely chopped gherkins or capers.
• Crushed, dried chillies or finely chopped fresh chillies.
• Crushed, fresh garlic cloves, or roasted garlic purée.
• Ground coriander seeds, curry spices or paste.

Savoury Egg Sauces

The versatility of eggs comes in useful in all kinds of sauces, most commonly for thickening and enriching cooked sauces, or for holding an emulsion such as in mayonnaise. Keep spare egg yolks in the freezer, ready to enrich sauces whenever needed – stir in a pinch of salt or sugar before freezing to prevent them from thickening.

Mayonnaise

The texture of a hand-whisked mayonnaise is quite unlike any other – smooth, glossy and rich, the perfect partner to delicately poached salmon or a chicken salad. The choice of oil for mayonnaise depends on personal taste, but most people would find mayonnaise made with extra virgin olive oil rather too powerful in flavour. So, it's a good idea to use either a pure olive oil, or alternatively use a mix of half pure olive oil with half sunflower oil, or another lighter-flavoured oil.

It is easier to get a good emulsion and prevent the mayonnaise curdling if all the ingredients are at room temperature.

Makes about 300ml/½ pint/1¼ cups

INGREDIENTS

2 egg yolks
15ml/1 tbsp lemon juice
5ml/1 tsp Dijon mustard
300ml/½ pint/1¼ cups light olive oil
salt and ground black pepper

1 Place the egg yolks, lemon juice, mustard, salt and pepper in a bowl and beat the egg yolk mixture until smooth and evenly combined.

2 Pouring with one hand and whisking with the other, add the oil gradually, drop by drop, making sure that each drop is whisked in before adding more.

3 Once a thick emulsion has formed, the oil can be poured faster, in a fine, steady stream, whisking until the mixture becomes smooth and thick. Adjust the seasoning to taste.

Using a Food Processor for Mayonnaise

A food processor can speed up the making of mayonnaise. Use a whole egg instead of the egg yolks.

Process the egg and flavourings for a few seconds then slowly pour in the oil through the feeder tube in a thin, steady stream with the motor running, until the mixture forms a smooth, creamy texture.

Preventing Mayonnaise from Separating

If the oil is added too quickly, the mayonnaise may separate, but this can be corrected if you work quickly.

Break a fresh egg yolk into a clean bowl. Gradually whisk in the separated mayonnaise, a small spoonful at a time, whisking constantly until it begins to thicken. Continue until all the mixture has been incorporated.

MAYONNAISE VARIATIONS

• For Garlic Mayonnaise, add in three to six crushed garlic cloves.
• For Spicy Mayonnaise, add in 15ml/1 tbsp mustard, 7–15ml/ ½–1 tsp Worcestershire sauce and a dash of Tabasco sauce.
• For Green Mayonnaise, combine 25g/1oz each parsley and watercress sprigs in a blender or food processor. Add three or four chopped spring onions (scallions) and one garlic clove. Blend until finely chopped. Add 120ml/4fl oz/½ cup mayonnaise and blend until smooth. Season to taste.
• For Blue Cheese Dressing, mix 225g/8oz crumbled Danish blue cheese into the mayonnaise.

Sweet Egg Sauces

Sweet egg sauces include many rich and creamy techniques, from classic egg-based custards to serve with winter puddings to light and fluffy sabayon which can be served on its own or as a luxurious sauce for gilded fruits, or traditional baked custard which can be served hot or cold.

Egg Custard Sauce

Crème anglaise is the traditional vanilla custard sauce made with eggs, a far cry from the quick custard powder versions so often used. As well as being served as a classic sauce, either hot or cold, *crème anglaise* is often used as the base for other sweet sauces, such as the *crème pâtissière* used to fill éclairs and profiteroles. It's frequently enriched with cream instead of milk, or flavoured with liqueurs for special desserts.

The trick here is to be patient – the egg must be cooked slowly; if it's overheated it will turn to scrambled egg.

Makes about 400ml/14fl oz/1⅔ cups

INGREDIENTS

300ml/½ pint /1¼ cups milk
1 vanilla pod (bean)
3 egg yolks
15ml/1 tbsp caster (superfine) sugar

1 Heat the milk with the vanilla pod until just boiling, then remove from the heat. (To intensify the flavour split the pod lengthways.) Cover and leave to infuse (steep) for 10 minutes then strain into a clean pan. Beat the eggs and sugar together lightly in a bowl.

2 Pour the milk on to the eggs, whisking constantly.

3 Pour into the pan and stir until the custard thickens just enough to coat the back of a wooden spoon. Remove from the heat and pour into a jug (pitcher) to prevent overcooking.

Preventing Curdling

Remove the pan from the heat and plunge the base into cold water. Whisk in a teaspoon of cornflour (corn-starch) until smooth, then reheat.

Sabayon Sauce

1 Whisk one egg yolk and 15ml/1 tbsp caster (superfine) sugar per portion in a bowl over a pan of simmering water. Whisk in 30ml/2 tbsp sweet white wine, liqueur or full-flavoured fruit juice, for each egg yolk. Whisk the sauce over a constant heat until frothy.

2 Whisk until the sauce holds a trail on top of the mixture. Serve immediately or whisk until cool.

Baked Custard

Preheat the oven to 180°C/350°F/ Gas 4. Grease an ovenproof dish. Beat together four large (US extra large) eggs, a few drops of vanilla essence (extract) and 15–30ml/1–2 tbsp caster sugar. Whisk in 600ml/1 pint/2½ cups hot milk, then strain into the dish. Stand the dish in a roasting pan half-filled with warm water. Bake for 50–60 minutes.

Dessert Sauces

As well as the popular custards and flavoured white sauces, quick and easy dessert toppings can be made almost instantly from ready-made ingredients, and these are ideal to serve over scoops of ice cream. They could also be served with pancakes and are particularly popular with children.

How to Use Vanilla Pods

Vanilla pods (beans) are commonly used in sweet dessert sauces, but they are occasionally used to flavour delicate savoury cream sauces.

To flavour sugar, bury a vanilla pod in a jar of caster (superfine) sugar. It can be used as vanilla-flavoured sugar to add to sweet sauces and desserts.

To infuse (steep) vanilla flavour into milk or cream, heat it gently with the vanilla pod over a low heat until almost boiling. Remove from the heat, cover and leave to stand for 10 minutes. Remove the pod, rinse and dry; it may be re-used several times in this way.

To get maximum flavour from the pod, use a sharp knife to slit the pod length-wise and open out. Use the tip of the knife to scrape out the sticky black seeds inside and add to the hot sauce.

Speedy Sauces for Topping Ice Cream

Lots of store-cupboard (pantry) ingredients can be quickly transformed into sauces to spoon on top of ice cream, so you'll always have a quick dessert.

Marshmallow Melt

Melt 90g/3½ oz marshmallows with 30ml/2 tbsp milk or cream in a small pan. Add a little grated nutmeg and spoon over ice cream.

Black Forest Sauce

Drain a can of black cherries, reserving the juice. Blend a little of the juice with a little arrowroot or cornflour (cornstarch). Add the cornflour mixture to the remaining juice in a pan. Stir over a moderate heat until boiling and lightly thickened, then add the cherries and a dash of kirsch. Bubble for a few seconds, then spoon over the ice cream and top with grated chocolate.

Chocolate-toffee Sauce

Chop a Mars (Heath) bar and heat gently in a pan, stirring until just melted. Spoon over scoops of vanilla ice cream and sprinkle with chopped nuts.

Marmalade Whisky Sauce

Heat 60ml/4 tbsp chunky marmalade in a pan with 30ml/2 tbsp whisky, until just melted. Allow to bubble for a few seconds then spoon over ice cream.

Whisky Sauce

Measure 600ml/1 pint/2½ cups milk. Mix together 30ml/2 tbsp cornflour (cornstarch) with 15ml/1 tbsp of the milk. Bring the remaining milk to a boil, remove from the heat and pour a little on the cornflour mixture. Return the mixture to the pan and heat gently, stirring constantly, until thickened. Simmer for 2 minutes.

Remove from the heat and stir in 30ml/2 tbsp caster (superfine) sugar and 60–90ml/4–6 tbsp whisky.

Presentation Ideas

When you've made a delicious sauce for a special dessert, why not make more of it by using it for decoration on the plate, too? Try one of the following simple ideas to make your sauce into a talking point. Individual slices of desserts, cakes or tarts, or a stuffed baked peach, look especially good like this.

Marbling

Use this technique when you have two contrasting sauces of similar thickness, such as a fruit purée with custard or cream. Spoon alternate spoonfuls of the sauces into a bowl or on to a serving plate, then stir the two sauces lightly together, swirling to create a marbled effect.

Yin-Yang Sauces

This is ideal for two contrasting colours of purée or coulis, such as a raspberry and a mango fruit coulis. Spoon one sauce on each side of a serving plate and push them together gently with a spoon, swirling one around the other, to make a yin-yang shape.

Drizzling

Pour a smooth sauce or coulis into a piping (pastry) bag with a fine pouring lip. Drizzle the sauce in droplets or a fine wavy line on to the plate around the food.

Piping Outlines

Spoon a small amount of fruit coulis or chocolate sauce into a piping bag with a plain writing nozzle. Pipe the outline of a shape on to a serving plate, then spoon in sauce to fill the inside.

Feathering Hearts

Flood the plate with a smooth sauce such as fruit purée. Add small droplets of pouring cream into it at intervals. Draw the tip of a small knife through the cream, to drag each drop into a heart.

Quick Sauces for Crêpes

Rich Butterscotch Sauce

Heat 75g/3oz/6 tbsp butter, 175g/6oz/1½ cups brown sugar and 30ml/2 tbsp golden (light corn) syrup in a pan over a low heat until melted. Remove from the heat and add 75ml/5 tbsp double (heavy) cream, stirring constantly, until smooth. If you like, add about 50g/2oz/½ cup chopped walnuts. Serve hot with ice cream and crêpes or waffles.

Orange Sauce

Melt 25g/1oz/2 tbsp unsalted (sweet) butter in a heavy pan. Stir in 50g/2oz/¼ cup caster (superfine) sugar and cook until golden. Add the juice of two oranges and half a lemon and stir until the caramel has dissolved.

Summer Berries

Melt 25g/1oz/2 tbsp butter in a frying pan. Add in 50g/2oz/¼ cup caster (superfine) sugar and cook until golden. Add the juice of two oranges and the rind of ½ orange and cook until syrupy. Add 350g/12oz/3 cups berries and heat. Add 45ml/3 tbsp Grand Marnier and set alight. Spoon over the crêpes.

Fruit Sauces

From the simplest fresh fruit purée, to a cooked and thickened fruit sauce, there are hundreds of ways to add flavour to desserts, tarts and pies. The addition of a little liqueur or lemon juice can bring out the fruit flavour and prevent discoloration. Some fruit sauces, notably apple and cranberry, partner meat and poultry dishes, and fresh fruit salsas can be eaten to cool down spicy hot dishes.

Making a Fruit Coulis

A delicious fruit coulis will add a sophisticated splash of colour and flavour to desserts and ices. It can be made from either fresh or frozen fruit, in any season. Soft fruits and berries such as raspberries, blackcurrants or strawberries are ideal, and tropical fruits like mango and kiwi fruit can be quickly transformed into exotically flavoured coulis. A few drops of orange flower water or rose water will give a scented flavour, but use it with caution – too much will overpower delicate ingredients.

| Remove any hulls, stems, peel or stones (pits) from the fruit.

2 Place the prepared fruit in a blender or food processor and process until smooth.

3 Press the purée through a fine sieve, to remove the pips (seeds) or fibrous parts. Sweeten to taste with icing (confectioners') sugar, and if necessary add a squeeze of lemon juice to sharpen the flavour.

COOK'S TIP

For cooked peeled fruit, mash with a potato masher for a coarser purée.

Peach Sauce

Purée a 400g/14oz can of peaches, together with their juice and 1.5ml/ ¼ tsp almond essence (extract) in a blender or food processor; chill the sauce before serving with fruit tarts or cakes.

Passion Fruit Coulis

Cut three ripe papayas in half and scoop out the seeds. Peel them and cut the flesh into chunks. Thread the chunks on bamboo skewers.

| Halve eight passion fruit and scoop out the flesh. Purée in a blender for a few seconds.

2 Press the pulp through a sieve and discard the seeds. Add 30ml/ 2 tbsp of lime juice, 30ml/2 tbsp of icing (confectioners') sugar and 30ml/2 tbsp of white rum. Stir well until the sugar has dissolved.

3 Spoon some of the coulis on to a serving plate. Place the skewers on top. Drizzle the remaining coulis over the skewers and garnish with a little toasted coconut, if you like.

Chocolate Sauces

Chocolate sauces are enduringly popular, from simple custards to richly indulgent versions combined with liqueur or cream. They can be served with ice cream and other frozen desserts, but are also delicious with poached pears and a wide range of puddings. Flavoured liqueurs can be chosen to echo the flavour of the dessert, and coffee, brandy and cinnamon all go especially well with chocolate.

The more cocoa solids chocolate contains, the stronger the flavour will be. Plain (semisweet) chocolate may have between 30–70 per cent of cocoa solids. Dark (bittersweet) chocolate has around 75 per cent, so if you're aiming for a really rich, dark sauce, this is the best choice. Milk chocolate is much sweeter, containing 20 per cent cocoa solids.

White chocolate contains no cocoa solids, so strictly speaking it is not a chocolate at all, but gets its flavour from cocoa butter.

The best method of melting chocolate is in a double boiler or in a bowl over a pan of hot water. Never allow water or steam to come into contact with the chocolate as this may cause it to stiffen. Overheating will also spoil the flavour and texture. Plain chocolate should not be heated above 49°C/120°F, and milk or white chocolate not above 43°C/110°F.

For sauce recipes where the chocolate is melted with a quantity of other liquid, such as milk or cream, the chocolate may be melted with the liquid in a pan over direct heat, providing there is plenty of liquid. Heat gently, stirring until melted.

Cocoa is ground from the whole cocoa mass after most of the cocoa butter has been extracted.

Creamy Chocolate Sauce

Place 120ml/4fl oz/½ cup double (heavy) cream in a pan and add 130g/4½oz chocolate pieces. Stir over a low heat until the chocolate has melted. Serve warm or cold.

COOK'S TIP

If you run out of chocolate for a sauce recipe, you can use unsweetened cocoa as a substitute. Mix 45ml/3 tbsp cocoa with 15ml/1 tbsp melted butter to replace each 25g/1oz chocolate.

Chocolate Custard Sauce

Melt 90g/3½oz dark (bittersweet) chocolate.

2 Heat 200ml/7fl oz/scant 1 cup *crème anglaise* until hot but not boiling and stir in the melted chocolate until evenly mixed. Serve hot or cold.

Rich Chocolate Brandy Sauce

Break up 115g/4oz plain (semisweet) chocolate into a bowl over a pan of hot water, then heat gently until melted. Remove from the heat and add 30ml/2 tbsp brandy and 30ml/2 tbsp melted butter, then stir until smooth. Serve hot.

Traditional Classic Sauces

Every country has its enduring time-honoured sauces, from
an Italian home-made Pesto Sauce or a French smooth
Velouté Sauce to British favourites such as Horseradish or
Bread Sauce. Each has evolved from the imaginative use of
local foods and has been created to enhance the flavours
of the traditional cuisine of the country. These tried and
tested classics form the basis of an essential repertoire
for every professional cook. They encompass all of the
sauce-making techniques, such as flour-thickened roux and
rich emulsions, and some of them form an integral part
of world-famous dishes.

Basic White Sauce

THIS WHITE SAUCE IS **wonderfully adaptable for all kinds of savoury dishes, but it can be bland so always taste and season carefully.**

Serves 6

INGREDIENTS

600ml/1 pint/2½ cups milk
25g/1oz/2 tbsp butter
25g/1oz/¼ cup plain (all-purpose) flour
salt and ground black pepper

1 Warm the milk in a pan over a low heat, but do not boil.

2 In a separate pan melt the butter, then stir in the flour and cook gently for 1–2 minutes to make a roux. Do not allow it to brown.

3 Remove the pan from the heat, gradually blend in the milk, stirring vigorously after each addition to prevent lumps forming.

4 Return to the heat and bring to the boil slowly, stirring constantly until the sauce thickens.

5 Simmer gently for a further 3–4 minutes until thickened and smooth. Season with salt and ground black pepper to taste.

COOK'S TIPS

• *For a thicker, coating sauce, increase the amount of flour to 50g/2oz/½ cup and the butter to 50g/2oz/¼ cup.*
• *If you aren't using a non-stick pan, use a small whisk to incorporate the flour and milk smoothly.*

VARIATIONS

• *Parsley sauce is traditionally served with bacon, fish and broad (fava) beans. Stir in 15ml/1 tbsp chopped fresh parsley just before serving.*
• *Cheese sauce makes delicious egg and vegetable gratins. Stir in 50g/2oz/½ cup finely grated mature (sharp) Cheddar and 2.5ml/½ tsp prepared mustard.*

Velouté Sauce

THIS SAVOURY POURING SAUCE is named after its smooth, velvety texture. It's based on a white stock made from fish, vegetables or meat, so it can easily be adapted to the dish you are serving.

Serves 4

INGREDIENTS

600ml/1 pint/2½ cups stock
25g/1oz/2 tbsp butter
25g/1oz/¼ cup plain (all-purpose) flour
30ml/2 tbsp single (light) cream
salt and ground black pepper

1 Heat the stock until almost boiling, but do not boil. In another pan melt the butter and stir in the flour. Cook, stirring, over a moderate heat for 3–4 minutes, or until a pale, straw colour, stirring constantly.

2 Remove the pan from the heat and gradually blend in the hot stock. Return to the heat and bring to the boil, stirring constantly, until the sauce thickens.

3 Continue to cook at a very slow simmer, stirring occasionally, until reduced by about one-quarter.

4 Skim the surface during cooking to remove any scum, or pour through a very fine strainer.

5 Just before serving, remove from the heat and stir in the cream. Season to taste.

VARIATION

For a richer flavour in a special dish, replace 30–45ml/2–3 tbsp of the stock with dry white wine or vermouth.

Lemon Sauce with Tarragon

THE SHARPNESS OF LEMON and the mild aniseed flavour of tarragon add zest to chicken, egg or steamed vegetable dishes.

Serves 4

INGREDIENTS

I lemon
a small bunch of fresh tarragon
I shallot, finely chopped
90ml/6 tbsp white wine
I quantity Velouté sauce
45ml/3 tbsp double (heavy) cream
30ml/2 tbsp brandy
salt and ground black pepper

I Thinly pare the rind from the lemon, taking care not to remove any of the white pith. Squeeze the juice from the lemon and pour it into a pan. Discard the lemon.

2 Discard the coarse stalks from the tarragon. Chop the leaves and add all but 15ml/1 tbsp to the pan with the lemon rind and shallot.

3 Add the wine and simmer gently until the liquid is reduced by half. Strain into a clean pan.

4 Add the Velouté sauce, cream, brandy and reserved tarragon. Heat through, taste and adjust the seasoning if necessary.

COOK'S TIP

This sauce goes well with pieces of boned chicken breast portions, wrapped with streaky (fatty) bacon rashers (strips) and grilled (broiled) or pan-fried.

Tangy Orange Sauce

KNOWN AS *SAUCE BIGARADE*, this is the perfect accompaniment for roast duckling and rich game. For a full mellow flavour it is best made with the rich roasting-pan juices.

Serves 4–6

INGREDIENTS

roasting-pan juices or 25g/1oz/
    2 tbsp butter
40g/1½oz/⅓ cup plain (all-purpose) flour
300ml/½ pint hot stock (preferably duck)
150ml/¼ pint/⅔ cup red wine
2 Seville (Temple) oranges or 2 sweet
    oranges plus 10ml/2 tsp lemon juice
15ml/1 tbsp orange-flavoured liqueur
30ml/2 tbsp redcurrant jelly
salt and ground black pepper

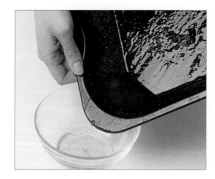

1 Carefully pour off any excess fat from the roasting pan, leaving the rich meat juices behind, or melt the butter in a small pan.

2 Sprinkle the flour into the juices or butter and cook, stirring constantly, for about 4 minutes, or until the mixture is lightly browned.

3 Off the heat, gradually blend in the hot stock and wine. Return to the heat and bring to the boil, stirring constantly. Lower the heat and simmer gently for 5 minutes.

4 Meanwhile, using a citrus zester, peel the rind thinly from one orange. Squeeze the juice from both of the oranges.

5 Place the rind in a small pan, cover with boiling water and bring back to the boil. Simmer for 5 minutes, then strain and add the rind to the sauce.

6 Add the orange juice to the sauce, along with the lemon juice, if using, and the liqueur and jelly. Stir until the jelly has dissolved. Season with salt and pepper to taste.

COOK'S TIP

Seville (Temple) oranges have a distinctive bitter flavour, which is good for savoury dishes, but they have a short season. They can be frozen whole, or you can freeze the juice and rind separately.

Hollandaise Sauce

A RICH BUTTER SAUCE rather like a
warm mayonnaise, is perfect for
steamed or grilled fish, such as
salmon, or vegetables such as
broccoli, asparagus or new potatoes.
The secret of success is patience.

Serves 2–3

INGREDIENTS

30ml/2 tbsp white wine or tarragon vinegar
15ml/1 tbsp water
6 black peppercorns
1 bay leaf
115g/4oz/½ cup butter
2 egg yolks
salt and ground black pepper
15–30ml/1–2 tbsp single (light)
   cream (optional)

1 Place the vinegar, water, peppercorns,
and bay leaf in a pan. Simmer the
liquid gently until it has reduced by half.
Strain and allow to cool.

2 In a separate bowl, cream the
butter until soft.

3 In a double boiler, or a heatproof
bowl sitting over a pan of gently
simmering, but not boiling, water, whisk
the egg yolks and infused (steeped)
vinegar liquid together gently until the
mixture is light and fluffy.

4 Gradually add the butter a tiny
piece at a time – about the size of
a hazelnut will be enough. Whisk
quickly until all the butter has been
absorbed before adding any more.

5 Season lightly and, if the sauce is
too sharp, add a little more butter.

6 For a thinner version of the sauce,
stir in some single cream. Serve
immediately.

COOK'S TIP

*Any leftover sauce can be stored in the
refrigerator for up to a week. Reheat very
gently in a bowl over simmering water,
whisking constantly.*

Rich Tomato Sauce

FOR A FULL TOMATO flavour and rich red colour, fresh Italian plum tomatoes are an excellent choice if they are available.

Serves 4–6

INGREDIENTS

30ml/2 tbsp olive oil
1 large onion, chopped
2 garlic cloves, crushed
1 carrot, finely chopped
1 celery stick, finely chopped
675g/1½lb tomatoes, peeled and chopped
150ml/¼ pint/⅔ cup red wine
150ml/¼ pint/⅔ cup vegetable stock
bouquet garni
2.5–5ml/½–1 tsp sugar
15ml/1 tbsp tomato purée (paste)
salt and ground black pepper

1 Heat the oil in a pan, add the onion and garlic and sauté until soft and pale golden brown. Add the carrot and celery and continue to cook, stirring occasionally, until golden.

2 Stir in the tomatoes, wine, stock and bouquet garni. Season with salt and ground black pepper to taste.

3 Bring the tomato mixture to the boil, then cover and simmer gently for 45 minutes, stirring occasionally to avoid burning. Remove the bouquet garni from the liquid, taste the sauce and adjust the seasoning, adding a pinch of sugar and tomato purée as necessary.

4 Serve the sauce as it is or, for a smoother texture, press through a sieve, or purée in a blender or food processor. This is delicious spooned over sliced courgettes (zucchini) or whole green beans.

Green Peppercorn Sauce

THIS SAUCE IS EXCELLENT with pasta, pork steaks or grilled chicken. The green peppercorns in brine are a better choice than the dry-packed type because they tend to give a more rounded flavour.

Serves 3–4

INGREDIENTS

15ml/1 tbsp green peppercorns in
   brine, drained
1 small onion, finely chopped
25g/1oz/2 tbsp butter
300ml/½ pint/1¼ cups light stock
juice of ½ lemon
15ml/1 tbsp beurre manié
45ml/3 tbsp double (heavy) cream
5ml/1 tsp Dijon mustard
salt and ground black pepper

1 Dry the peppercorns on absorbent kitchen paper, then crush lightly under the blade of a heavy-duty knife or use a mortar and pestle.

2 Soften the onion in the butter, add the stock and lemon juice and simmer for 15 minutes.

3 Whisk in the beurre manié a little at a time and continue to cook, stirring, until the sauce thickens.

VARIATION

For a lighter, less rich sauce, use crème fraîche instead of the double cream.

4 Reduce the heat and stir in the peppercorns, cream and mustard. Heat until boiling then season to taste. Serve hot with buttered pasta or the dish of your choice.

COOK'S TIP

For beurre manié, knead together equal quantities of butter and flour.

Quick Satay Sauce

THERE ARE MANY VERSIONS of this tasty peanut sauce. This one is very speedy and it tastes delicious drizzled over grilled or barbecued skewers of chicken. For parties, spear chunks of chicken with cocktail sticks and arrange around a bowl of sauce.

Serves 4

INGREDIENTS

200ml/7fl oz/scant 1 cup coconut cream
60ml/4 tbsp crunchy peanut butter
1 tsp Worcestershire sauce
Tabasco sauce, to taste
fresh coconut, to garnish (optional)

1 Pour the coconut cream into a small pan and heat it gently over a low heat for about 2 minutes.

2 Add the peanut butter and stir vigorously until it is blended into the coconut cream. Continue to heat until the mixture is warm but not boiling hot.

3 Add the Worcestershire sauce and a dash of Tabasco to taste. Pour into a serving bowl.

COOK'S TIP

Thick coconut milk can be substituted for coconut cream, but take care to buy an unsweetened variety for this recipe.

4 Use a potato peeler to shave thin curls from a piece of fresh coconut, if using. Sprinkle the coconut over the dish of your choice and serve immediately with the sauce.

Pesto Sauce

THERE IS NOTHING MORE evocative of the warmth of Italy than a good home-made pesto. Serve in generous spoonfuls with your favourite pasta.

Serves 3–4

INGREDIENTS

50g/2oz/1 cup basil leaves
2 garlic cloves, crushed
30ml/2 tbsp pine nuts
120ml/4fl oz/½ cup olive oil
40g/1½oz/½ cup finely grated fresh
   Parmesan cheese
salt and ground black pepper

Using a food processor: Place the basil, garlic, pine nuts and seasoning in the food processor and process as finely as possible.

2 With the machine running slowly add the oil in a thin stream, combining the ingredients until they have formed a smooth paste.

3 Add the cheese and pulse quickly three or four times. Adjust the seasoning if necessary and heat gently.

VARIATION

Pesto makes an excellent dressing for boiled new potatoes. Serve while hot or allow to cool to room temperature.

By hand: Using a mortar and pestle, grind the basil, garlic, pine nuts and seasoning to a fine paste.

2 Transfer the mixture to a bowl and whisk in the oil a little at a time.

3 Add the cheese and blend well. Adjust the seasoning to taste and heat the sauce gently.

Barbecue Sauce

BRUSH THIS SAUCE OVER chops, kebabs or chicken drumsticks before cooking on the barbecue, or serve as a hot or cold accompaniment to hot dogs and burgers.

Serves 4

INGREDIENTS

30ml/2 tbsp vegetable oil
1 large onion, chopped
2 garlic cloves, crushed
400g/14oz can tomatoes
30ml/2 tbsp Worcestershire sauce
15ml/1 tbsp white wine vinegar
45ml/3 tbsp honey
5ml/1 tsp mustard powder
2.5ml/½ tsp chilli seasoning or mild chilli powder
salt and ground black pepper

1 In a pan, heat the oil and fry the onion and garlic until soft.

2 Stir in the remaining ingredients and bring to the boil. Simmer, uncovered, for 15–20 minutes, stirring occasionally. Cool slightly.

3 Pour into a food processor or blender and process until smooth.

4 Press the sauce through a sieve if you prefer a smoother result, and adjust the seasoning with salt and pepper to taste before serving.

VARIATION

For a really rich, spicy chilli flavour, omit the chilli seasoning and instead add a small red chilli, seeded and chopped. Leave the seeds in if you like it really hot.

Apple Sauce

REALLY MORE OF A condiment than a sauce, this tart purée is usually served cold or warm, rather than hot. It's typically served with rice, roast pork or duck, but is also good with cold meats and savoury pies.

Serves 6

INGREDIENTS
225g/8oz tart cooking apples
30ml/2 tbsp water
thin strip of lemon rind
15ml/1 tbsp butter
15–30ml/1–2 tbsp caster (superfine) sugar

3 Remove the lemon rind from the pan and discard. Beat the apples to a pulp with a spoon, or press through a sieve.

4 Stir the butter into the apple sauce and then add sugar to taste.

VARIATIONS

• *To make a Normandy Apple Sauce, try stirring in 15ml/1 tbsp Calvados with the butter and sugar at step 4.*
• *To make a creamy savoury apple sauce, stir in 30ml/2 tbsp sour cream or crème fraîche at step 4.*

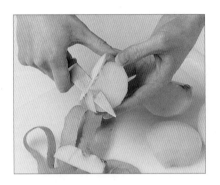

1 Peel the apples, cut into quarters and remove the core. Cut into thin, even slices.

2 Place the apples in a pan with the water and lemon rind. Cook, uncovered, over a low heat until very soft, stirring occasionally.

Mint Sauce

TART, YET SWEET, this simple sauce is the perfect foil to rich meat. It's best served, of course, with the new season's tender roast lamb, but it is also wonderful with grilled lamb chops or pan-fried duck.

Serves 6

INGREDIENTS
small bunch of mint
15ml/1 tbsp sugar
30ml/2 tbsp boiling water
45ml/3 tbsp white wine vinegar

1 Strip the mint leaves from the stalks and finely chop the leaves.

2 Place in a bowl with the sugar and pour on the boiling water. Stir well and allow the mixture to stand for 5–10 minutes.

3 Add the vinegar and leave to stand for 1–2 hours before serving.

COOK'S TIP

This sauce also makes a refreshing dressing to enhance the summery flavour of fresh peas or new potatoes.

Cranberry Sauce

THIS IS THE TRADITIONAL sauce for roast turkey, but don't keep it just for festive occasions. The vibrant colour and tart taste are a perfect partner to any white roast meat, and it makes a great addition to a chicken or Brie sandwich.

Serves 6

INGREDIENTS
1 orange
225g/8oz/2 cups cranberries
250g/9oz/1¼ cups caster (superfine) sugar
150ml/¼ pint/⅔ cup water

1 Pare the rind thinly from the orange using a swivel-bladed vegetable peeler, taking care not to remove any white pith. Squeeze the juice.

2 Place in a pan with the cranberries, sugar and water.

3 Bring to a boil, stirring until the sugar has dissolved, then allow to simmer gently for 10–15 minutes or until the berries burst.

4 Remove the orange rind and allow to cool before serving.

COOK'S TIP

Fresh or frozen cranberries may be used in this sauce, depending on the season. Use fresh as a first choice.

Horseradish Sauce

THIS LIGHT, CREAMY SAUCE has a peppery flavour that's spiced with just a hint of mustard. It is the classic accompaniment to roast beef, but is perfect, too, with herby sausages and grilled fish, especially oily fish such as mackerel.

Serves 6

INGREDIENTS
7.5cm/3in piece fresh horseradish
15ml/1 tbsp lemon juice
10ml/2 tsp sugar
2.5ml/½ tsp English (hot) mustard powder
150ml/¼ pint/⅔ cup double (heavy) cream

1 | Scrub and peel the piece of fresh horseradish, and then grate it as finely as possible.

2 In a bowl, mix together the grated horseradish, lemon juice, sugar and mustard powder.

3 Whip the cream until it stands in soft peaks, then gently fold in the horseradish mixture.

VARIATION

For a change of flavour, replace the lemon juice with tarragon vinegar.

Bread Sauce

SMOOTH AND SURPRISINGLY DELICATE, this old-fashioned sauce dates back to medieval times. It's traditionally served with roast chicken, turkey and game birds.

Serves 6

INGREDIENTS
1 small onion
4 cloves
bay leaf
300ml/½ pint/1¼ cups milk
90g/3½ oz/scant 2 cups fresh
   white breadcrumbs
15ml/1 tbsp butter
15ml/1 tbsp single (light) cream
salt and ground black pepper

1 | Peel the onion and stick the cloves into it. Put it into a pan with the bay leaf and pour in the milk.

2 Bring to the boil, then remove from the heat and allow to infuse (steep) for 15–20 minutes. Remove the bay leaf and onion from the milk.

3 Return to the heat and stir in the breadcrumbs. Simmer for 4–5 minutes, or until thick and creamy.

4 Stir in the butter and cream, then season to taste.

COOK'S TIP

If you would prefer a less strong flavour, reduce the number of cloves in the onion to one or two and add a little freshly grated nutmeg to the milk instead.

Sauces for Pasta Dishes

Most pasta sauces are refreshingly simple and foolproof, and
do not need hours of preparation. Many of these sauces are
designed to match particular types or shapes of pasta, but
will work well with other types of pasta, so try experimenting
with your favourites. It's rare for a pasta sauce to be
flour-thickened, but some are enriched or thickened with
eggs, such as carbonara. Those that are simmered for long
periods, such as Bolognese sauce, reach a thicker consistency
as they are reduced and become more concentrated.
There are also sauces that are wonderfully easy to make,
and may be as simple as butter and herbs.

Sun-dried Tomato and Radicchio Sauce with Paglia e Fieno

THIS IS A LIGHT, MODERN pasta dish of the kind served in fashionable restaurants. It is the presentation that sets it apart. It is very quick and easy to prepare.

Serves 4

INGREDIENTS

45ml/3 tbsp pine nuts
350g/12oz paglia e fieno pasta
30ml/2 tbsp extra virgin olive oil
4–6 spring onions (scallions), thinly sliced
   into rings

**For the sun-dried tomato and
   radicchio sauce**
15ml/1 tbsp extra virgin olive oil
30ml/2 tbsp sun-dried tomato paste
40g/1½oz radicchio leaves, finely shredded
salt and ground black pepper

1 Put the pine nuts in a heavy frying pan and toss over a medium heat for 1–2 minutes until lightly toasted and golden brown. Remove and set aside.

2 Cook the pasta according to the packet instructions, keeping the colours separate by using two pans.

3 To make the sauce, heat the oil in a medium frying pan. Add the sun-dried tomato paste, then stir in two ladlefuls of pasta cooking water. Simmer until the sauce is slightly reduced, stirring constantly.

4 Stir in the shredded radicchio, then taste and season. Keep on a low heat. Drain the pasta, keeping the colours separate, and return them to the pans in which they were cooked. Add 15ml/1 tbsp of oil to each pan and toss over a medium to high heat until the pasta is glistening.

5 Arrange a portion of green and white pasta in each of four warmed bowls, then spoon the sun-dried tomato and radicchio sauce in the centre. Sprinkle the spring onions and toasted pine nuts decoratively over the top and serve immediately. Before eating, each diner should toss the sauce with the pasta to mix well.

COOK'S TIP

If you find the presentation too fussy, you can toss the sun-dried tomato and radicchio mixture with the pasta in one large warmed bowl before serving, then sprinkle with spring onions and pine nuts.

Tomato and Chilli Sauce with Pasta

THIS IS A SPECIALITY OF LAZIO in Italy
– the Italian name for the sauce,
al arrabbiata, means rabid or angry,
and describes its heat.

Serves 4

INGREDIENTS

300g/11oz dried penne or tortiglioni

For the tomato and chilli sauce
500g/1¼lb sugocasa
2 garlic cloves, crushed
150ml/¼ pint/⅔ cup dry white wine
15ml/1 tbsp sun-dried tomato paste
1 fresh red chilli
30ml/2 tbsp finely chopped fresh flat leaf
*   parsley, plus extra to garnish*
salt and ground black pepper
grated fresh Pecorino cheese, to serve

1 Put the sugocasa, garlic, wine, tomato
paste and whole chilli in a pan and
bring to the boil. Cover and simmer
over a low heat.

2 Drop the pasta into a large pan of
rapidly boiling lightly salted water
and cook for 10–12 minutes, or until
al dente.

3 Remove the chilli from the sauce
and add the parsley. Taste for
seasoning. If you prefer a hotter taste,
chop some or all of the chilli and
return it to the sauce.

4 Drain the pasta and tip into a
warmed large bowl. Pour the sauce
over the pasta and toss to mix. Serve
at once, sprinkled with parsley and
grated Pecorino.

COOK'S TIPS

• *If you prefer the flavour to be slightly
less hot, remove the seeds from the chilli
before using. Split the chilli down its
length and scrape out the fiery seeds
with the tip of a knife.*
• *Sugocasa literally means "house
sauce" and consists of tomatoes,
crushed coarsely so that they have a
chunky texture.*

Clam and Tomato Sauce with Vermicelli

CLAM AND TOMATO SAUCE is a regular dish in Neopolitan restaurants, and is often served with vermicelli or spaghetti. Fresh mussels could be substituted for the clams.

Serves 4

INGREDIENTS
350g/12oz vermicelli

For the clam and tomato sauce
1kg/2¼lb fresh hard-shell clams
250ml/8fl oz/1 cup dry white wine
2 garlic cloves, bruised
1 large handful fresh flat leaf parsley
30ml/2 tbsp olive oil
1 small onion, finely chopped
8 ripe plum tomatoes, peeled, seeded and finely chopped
½–1 fresh red chilli, seeded and finely chopped
salt and ground black pepper

1 Scrub the clams thoroughly under cold running water and discard any that are open and that do not close when they are sharply tapped against the work surface.

2 Pour the wine into a large pan, add the garlic cloves and half the parsley, then the clams. Cover tightly with the lid and bring to the boil over a high heat. Cook for about 5 minutes, shaking the pan frequently, until the clams have opened.

3 Tip the clams into a large colander set over a bowl and let the liquid drain through. Set aside the clams until cool enough to handle, then remove about two-thirds of them from their shells, pouring the clam liquid into the bowl of cooking liquid. Discard any clams that have failed to open. Set both shelled and unshelled clams aside, keeping the unshelled clams warm in a bowl covered with a lid.

4 Heat the oil in a pan, add the onion and cook gently, stirring frequently, for about 5 minutes until softened and lightly coloured. Add the tomatoes, then strain in the clam cooking liquid. Add the chilli and salt and pepper to taste. Chop the remaining parsley finely and set aside.

5 Bring to the boil, half-cover the pan and allow to simmer gently for 15–20 minutes.

6 Meanwhile, cook the pasta according to the instructions on the packet, until it is *al dente*.

7 Add the shelled clams to the tomato sauce, stir well and heat through very gently for 2–3 minutes.

8 Drain the cooked pasta well and tip it into a warmed bowl. Taste the sauce for seasoning, then pour the sauce over the pasta and toss everything together well. Serve garnished with the reserved clams and sprinkled with parsley.

Carbonara Sauce with Spaghetti

AN ALL-TIME FAVOURITE sauce that is perfect for spaghetti or tagliatelle. This version has plenty of pancetta or bacon and is not too creamy, but you can vary the amounts.

Serves 4

INGREDIENTS

350g/12oz fresh or dried spaghetti

For the carbonara sauce
30ml/2 tbsp olive oil
1 small onion, finely chopped
8 pancetta or lean bacon, cut into
 1cm/¹/₂ in strips
4 eggs
60ml/4 tbsp crème fraîche
60ml/4 tbsp freshly grated Parmesan
 cheese, plus extra to serve
salt and ground black pepper

1 Heat the oil in a frying pan, add the onion and cook, stirring, over a low heat, for 5 minutes until softened.

2 Add the strips of pancetta or bacon to the onion in the pan and cook for about 10 minutes, stirring almost all the time.

3 Meanwhile, cook the pasta in a pan of salted boiling water according to the instructions on the packet, until *al dente*.

4 Put the eggs, crème fraîche and grated Parmesan in a bowl. Grind in plenty of pepper, then beat the mixture together well.

5 Drain the pasta, turn it into the pan with the pancetta or bacon and toss well to mix.

6 Turn the heat off under the pan. Immediately add the egg mixture and toss vigorously so that it cooks lightly and coats the pasta.

7 Quickly taste for seasoning, then divide among four warmed bowls and sprinkle with black pepper. Serve immediately, with extra grated Parmesan offered separately.

Cannelloni with Two Sauces

41

THE COMBINATION OF THE full-flavoured tomato sauce and the creamy white sauce makes this cannelloni dish a success. For a special occasion, make it in advance to the baking stage. Add the white sauce and bake on the day.

Serves 6

INGREDIENTS

15ml/1 tbsp olive oil
1 small onion, finely chopped
450g/1lb minced (ground) beef
1 garlic clove, finely chopped
5ml/1 tsp dried mixed herbs
120ml/4fl oz/½ cup beef stock
1 egg
75g/3oz cooked ham or mortadella
   sausage, finely chopped
45ml/3 tbsp fine fresh white breadcrumbs
115g/4oz/1¼ cups freshly grated
   Parmesan cheese
18 precooked cannelloni tubes
salt and ground black pepper

For the tomato sauce

30ml/2 tbsp olive oil
1 small onion, finely chopped
½ carrot, finely chopped
1 celery stick, finely chopped
1 garlic clove, crushed
400g/14oz can chopped plum tomatoes
a few sprigs of fresh basil
2.5ml/½ tsp dried oregano

For the white sauce

50g/2oz/¼ cup butter
50g/2oz/½ cup plain (all-purpose) flour
900ml/1½ pints/3¾ cups milk
fresh nutmeg

1 Heat the olive oil in a pan and cook the chopped onion over a gentle heat, stirring occasionally, for about 5 minutes, until softened.

2 Add the minced beef and garlic and cook for 10 minutes, stirring and breaking up any lumps with a wooden spoon.

3 Add the herbs, and season to taste, then moisten with half the stock. Cover the pan and allow to simmer for 25 minutes, stirring occasionally and adding more stock as it reduces. Spoon into a bowl and allow to cool.

4 To make the tomato sauce, heat the olive oil in a pan, add the vegetables and garlic and cook over a medium heat, stirring frequently, for 10 minutes. Add the tomatoes. Fill the empty can with water, pour it into the pan, then add the herbs, and season to taste. Bring to a boil, lower the heat, cover and simmer for 25–30 minutes, stirring occasionally. Purée the tomato sauce in a blender or food processor.

5 To the meat, add the egg, ham or mortadella, breadcrumbs and 90ml/6 tbsp of the grated Parmesan, and stir well to mix. Taste for seasoning.

6 Spread a little of the tomato sauce over the bottom of a rectangular ovenproof dish. Using a teaspoon, fill the cannelloni with the meat mixture.

7 Place the cannelloni in a single layer on top of the sauce. Pour the remaining tomato sauce over the top.

8 Preheat the oven to 190°C/375°F/ Gas 5. For the white sauce, melt the butter in pan, add the flour and cook for 1–2 minutes. Remove from the heat and blend in the milk.

9 Return to the heat, bring to the boil and stir until smooth and thick. Grate in fresh nutmeg, and season.

10 Pour over the cannelloni, then sprinkle with Parmesan. Bake for 40–45 minutes. Leave to stand for 10 minutes before serving.

Butter and Herb Sauce with Chitarra Spaghetti

YOU CAN USE JUST one favourite herb or several for this recipe. The result is the simplest way to dress up pasta but also one of the tastiest.

Serves 4

INGREDIENTS

400g/14oz fresh or dried spaghetti
*   alla chitarra*
freshly grated Parmesan cheese, to serve

For the butter and herb sauce
2 good handfuls mixed fresh herbs, plus
*   extra herb leaves and flowers to garnish*
115g/4oz/½ cup butter
salt and ground black pepper

1 Cook the pasta in boiling, lightly salted water according to the packet instructions, until almost *al dente*.

2 To make the sauce, chop the herbs coarsely or finely, as you prefer.

3 When the pasta is almost *al dente*, melt the butter in a large pan. As soon as it sizzles, drain the pasta and add it to the pan, then sprinkle in the herbs with salt and pepper to taste.

4 Toss over a medium heat until the pasta is coated in butter and herbs. Serve immediately in warmed bowls, sprinkled with extra herb leaves and flowers. Pass round some extra grated Parmesan separately.

VARIATION

If you like the flavour of garlic with herbs, add one or two crushed garlic cloves when melting the butter.

Bolognese Sauce with Ravioli

PERHAPS ONE OF THE most famous pasta sauces outside Italy, Bolognese sauce is a rich ragoût from the city of Bologna in Emilia-Romagna, an area famous for fine foods.

Serves 6

INGREDIENTS
225g/8oz cottage cheese
30ml/2 tbsp freshly grated Parmesan
   cheese, plus extra for serving
1 egg white, beaten, including extra
   for brushing
1.5ml/¼ tsp ground nutmeg
300g/11oz fresh pasta dough
flour, for dusting
salt and ground black pepper

For the Bolognese sauce
1 medium onion, finely chopped
1 garlic clove, crushed
150ml/¼ pint/⅔ cup beef stock
350g/12oz minced (ground) extra-lean beef
120ml/4fl oz/½ cup red wine
30ml/2 tbsp concentrated tomato
   purée (paste)
400g/14oz can chopped plum tomatoes
2.5ml/½ tsp chopped fresh rosemary
1.5ml/¼ tsp ground allspice

1 To make the filling, mix the cottage cheese, Parmesan, egg white, seasoning and nutmeg together.

2 Roll the pasta into thin sheets, then place small amounts of filling along the pasta in rows, leaving a gap of 5cm/2in between them. Moisten round the filling with beaten egg white.

3 Place a second sheet of pasta lightly over the top. Press between each pocket to remove air, and seal.

4 Cut into rounds with a fluted ravioli or pastry cutter. Transfer to a floured dishtowel and leave to rest for at least 30 minutes before cooking.

5 To make the Bolognese sauce, cook the onion and garlic in the stock for 5 minutes or until all the stock has reduced. Add the beef and cook quickly to brown, breaking up the meat with a fork.

VARIATION

Stir in a handful of chopped chicken livers with the minced beef to add a more meaty richness to the sauce.

6 Add the wine, tomato purée, chopped tomatoes, rosemary and allspice. Bring to the boil and simmer for 1 hour. Season to taste.

7 Cook the ravioli in a large pan of boiling, salted water for 4–5 minutes. (Cook in batches to stop them sticking together.) Drain thoroughly. Serve topped with the Bolognese sauce. Serve grated Parmesan cheese separately.

Spinach Sauce with Seafood Pasta Shells

SOFT CHEESE AND SPINACH complements all kinds of pasta. This sauce would be perfect with any filled fresh pasta.

Serves 4

INGREDIENTS

32 large dried pasta shells
salt and ground black pepper

For the filling
15g/½oz/1 tbsp butter or margarine
8 spring onions (scallions), thinly sliced
6 tomatoes
225g/8oz cooked peeled prawns (shrimp)
175g/6oz can white crab meat, drained and flaked

For the spinach sauce
225g/8oz/1 cup soft cheese
90ml/6 tbsp milk
pinch of freshly grated nutmeg
115g/4oz frozen chopped spinach, thawed and drained
salt and ground black pepper

1 Preheat the oven to 150°C/300°F/Gas 2. Melt the butter or margarine in a pan and cook the spring onions for 3–4 minutes, or until soft.

2 Plunge the tomatoes into boiling water for 1 minute, then into cold water. Slip off the skins. Halve the tomatoes, remove the seeds and cores and roughly chop the flesh.

3 Cook the pasta shells in lightly salted boiling water for about 10 minutes, or until *al dente*. Drain.

4 To make the sauce, put the soft cheese and milk into a pan and heat gently, stirring until blended. Season with salt, ground black pepper and a pinch of nutmeg.

5 Measure 30ml/2 tbsp of cheese mixture into a bowl. Add the onions, tomatoes, prawns, and crab meat. Mix well. Spoon the filling into the shells and place in a single layer in a shallow ovenproof dish. Cover with foil and cook for 10 minutes.

6 Stir the spinach into the remaining sauce. Bring to the boil and simmer gently for 1 minute, stirring constantly. Serve hot, drizzled over pasta.

Smoked Haddock and Parsley Sauce for Pasta

THIS HEARTY SAUCE made with smoked haddock makes any hollow pasta shape into a healthy lunch or supper. Shell-shaped pasta is ideal to hold the sauce, but corkscrew and tube shapes work just as well.

Serves 4

INGREDIENTS
225g/8oz pasta shells
15g/¹/₂oz toasted flaked (sliced) almonds, to serve

For the smoked haddock and parsley sauce
450g/1lb smoked haddock fillet
1 small leek or onion, thickly sliced
300ml/¹/₂ pint/1¼ cups milk
bouquet garni
25g/1oz/2 tbsp butter or margarine
25g/1oz/¼ cup plain (all-purpose) flour
30ml/2 tbsp chopped fresh parsley
salt and ground black pepper

1 Remove all the skin and any bones from the haddock and discard. Put the fish into a pan with the leek or onion, milk and bouquet garni. Bring to the boil, cover and simmer gently for 8–10 minutes, or until the fish flakes easily.

2 Strain, reserving the milk for making the sauce, and discard the bouquet garni.

3 Put the butter or margarine, flour and reserved milk into a pan. Bring to the boil and whisk until smooth. Season and add the fish and leek or onion.

4 Cook the pasta in a large pan of boiling salted water until *al dente*. Drain thoroughly and stir into the sauce with the chopped parsley. Serve immediately, sprinkled with toasted flaked almonds.

Prawn and Vodka Sauce with Pasta

THE COMBINATION OF PRAWNS , vodka and pasta may seem unusual, but has become a modern classic in Italy. Here it is served with two-coloured pasta, but the sauce goes equally well with short shapes.

Serves 4

INGREDIENTS
350g/12oz fresh or dried paglia e fieno

For the prawn and vodka sauce
30ml/2 tbsp olive oil
¼ large onion, finely chopped
1 garlic clove, crushed
15–30ml/1–2 tbsp sun-dried tomato paste
200ml/7fl oz/1 cup double (heavy) cream
12 large raw prawns (shrimp), peeled and chopped
30ml/2 tbsp vodka
salt and ground black pepper

1 Heat the oil in a medium pan, add the onion and garlic and cook gently, stirring frequently, for about 5 minutes or until softened.

2 Add the tomato paste and stir for 1–2 minutes, then add the cream and bring to the boil, stirring. Season with salt and pepper to taste and let the sauce bubble until it starts to thicken slightly. Remove from the heat.

3 Cook the pasta according to the instructions on the packet, until al dente. When it is almost ready, add the prawns and vodka to the sauce; toss over a medium heat for 2–3 minutes, or until the prawns turn pink.

4 Drain the pasta and turn it into a warmed bowl. Pour the sauce over and toss well. Divide among warmed bowls and serve immediately.

COOK'S TIP

This sauce is best served as soon as it is ready, otherwise the prawns will overcook and become tough. Make sure that the pasta has only a minute or two of cooking time left before adding the prawns to the sauce.

Smoked Salmon and Cream Sauce with Penne

THIS MODERN WAY OF serving pasta is popular all over Italy. The three essential ingredients combine beautifully, and the dish is very quick and easy to make.

Serves 4

INGREDIENTS
350g/12oz penne

For the smoked salmon and cream sauce
115g/4oz thinly sliced smoked salmon
2–3 fresh thyme sprigs
25g/1oz/2 tbsp butter
150ml/¼ pint/⅔ cup double (heavy) cream
salt and ground black pepper

1 Cook the pasta in boiling salted water until it is al dente.

2 Meanwhile, using kitchen scissors, cut the smoked salmon into thin strips, about 5mm/¼in wide. Strip the leaves from the thyme sprigs.

3 Melt the butter in a large pan. Stir in the cream with one-quarter of the salmon and thyme leaves, then season with pepper. Heat gently for 3–4 minutes, stirring constantly. Do not allow to boil. Taste for seasoning.

4 Drain the pasta and toss it in the cream and salmon sauce. Divide among four warmed bowls and top with the remaining salmon and thyme leaves. Serve immediately.

VARIATION

Although penne is traditional with this sauce, it also goes very well with fresh ravioli stuffed with spinach and ricotta.

Spicy Sausage Sauce with Tortiglioni

SERVE THIS HEADY PASTA DISH with a robust Sicilian red wine.

Serves 4

INGREDIENTS

300g/11oz dried tortiglioni
salt and ground black pepper

For the spicy sausage sauce

30ml/2 tbsp olive oil
1 onion, finely chopped
1 celery stick, finely chopped
2 large garlic cloves, crushed
1 fresh red chilli, seeded and chopped
450g/1lb ripe plum tomatoes, peeled and finely chopped
30ml/2 tbsp tomato purée (paste)
150ml/¼ pint/⅔ cup red wine
5ml/1 tsp sugar
175g/6oz spicy salami, rind removed
30ml/2 tbsp chopped parsley, to garnish
freshly grated Parmesan cheese, to serve

1 Heat the oil in a flameproof casserole or large pan, then add the onion, celery, garlic and chilli. Cook gently, stirring frequently, for about 10 minutes, until softened.

2 Add the tomatoes, tomato purée, wine, sugar and salt and pepper to taste and bring to the boil, stirring. Lower the heat, cover and simmer gently, stirring occasionally, for about 20 minutes. Add a few spoonfuls of water if the sauce becomes too thick.

3 Meanwhile, cook the pasta in a large pan of rapidly boiling, salted water according to the instructions on the packet, until *al dente*.

4 Chop the salami into bitesize chunks and add to the sauce. Heat through, then taste for seasoning.

5 Drain the pasta, tip it into a large bowl, then pour the sauce over and toss to mix. Sprinkle over the parsley and serve with grated Parmesan.

COOK'S TIP

Buy the salami for this dish in one piece so that you can chop it into large chunks.

Wild Mushroom Sauce with Fusilli

A VERY RICH DISH with an earthy flavour and lots of garlic, this makes an ideal main course for vegetarians, especially if it is followed by a crisp green salad.

Serves 4

INGREDIENTS

150g/5oz wild mushrooms preserved in olive oil
30ml/2 tbsp butter
150g/5oz fresh wild mushrooms, sliced if large
5ml/1 tsp finely chopped fresh thyme
5ml/1 tsp finely chopped fresh marjoram or oregano, plus extra herbs to serve
4 garlic cloves, crushed
350g/12oz fresh or dried fusilli
200ml/7fl oz/scant 1 cup double (heavy) cream
salt and ground black pepper

1 Drain about 15ml/1 tbsp of the oil from the mushrooms into a medium pan. Slice the preserved mushrooms into bitesize pieces, if they are large.

2 Add the butter to the oil in the pan and heat over a low heat until sizzling. Add the preserved and the fresh mushrooms, the chopped herbs and the garlic. Season to taste.

SAFETY TIP

Unless you're an expert, or know of one who will identify them for you, it's safer not to pick mushrooms in the wild, but buy them instead from a reliable source.

3 Simmer over a medium heat, stirring frequently, for about 10 minutes or until the fresh mushrooms are soft and tender.

4 Meanwhile, cook the pasta in boiling salted water according to the packet instructions, until *al dente*.

5 As soon as the mushrooms are cooked, increase the heat to high and toss the mixture with a wooden spoon to boil off any excess liquid. Pour in the cream and bring to the boil. Season if necessary.

6 Drain the pasta and turn it into a warmed bowl. Pour the sauce over and toss well. Serve immediately, sprinkled with chopped fresh herbs.

Sauces for Meat Dishes

Many red meat dishes provide the opportunity for quite robust sauces, using warm spices, garlic or pungent herbs, simmered with red wine or tomato mixtures for added richness. The contrasting flavours of tangy fruits are particularly successful with rich meats, such as the combination of Avocado Sauce with Lemon Chicken, and Walnut and Pomegranate Sauce with Duck Breasts. Pork is also a natural partner for the tangy sweetness of apples or oranges. More delicately flavoured white meats or poultry, such as chicken and turkey, go well with cream sauces or sauces based on white wine.

Marsala Cream Sauce with Turkey

MARSALA MAKES A VERY rich and tasty sauce. The addition of lemon juice gives it a refreshing tang, which helps to offset the richness.

Serves 6

INGREDIENTS

6 turkey breast steaks
45ml/3 tbsp plain (all-purpose) flour
30ml/2 tbsp olive oil
25g/1oz/2 tbsp butter
salt and ground black pepper

For the Marsala cream sauce
175ml/6fl oz/¾ cup dry Marsala
60ml/4 tbsp lemon juice
175ml/6fl oz/¾ cup double (heavy) cream

To serve
lemon wedges and chopped fresh parsley,
   to garnish
mangetouts (snow peas) and green beans

1 Put each turkey steak between two sheets of clear film (plastic wrap) and pound with a rolling pin to flatten. Cut each steak in half or into quarters, discarding any sinew.

2 Spread out the flour in a shallow bowl. Season well with salt and pepper and coat the meat.

3 Heat the oil and butter in a wide, heavy pan until sizzling. Add as many pieces of turkey as you can, and sauté over a medium heat for about 3 minutes on each side until crispy and tender.

4 Transfer to a warmed serving dish with tongs and keep hot. Repeat with the remaining turkey. Lower the heat.

5 To make the sauce, mix the Marsala and lemon juice in a jug (pitcher), add to the oil and butter in the pan and raise the heat. Bring to the boil, stirring in the sediment, then add the cream.

6 Simmer, stirring constantly, until the sauce is reduced and glossy. Taste for seasoning.

7 Spoon the sauce over the turkey, garnish with the lemon wedges and parsley and serve with the vegetables.

COOK'S TIP

To make this sauce without using the pan drippings, omit the oil and heat the butter in a pan before adding the other ingredients.

Avocado Sauce with Lemon Chicken

THIS GREAT SAUCE IS based on the classic Mexican dip, guacamole. Made without the addition of water, it could be used as a dip with raw vegetables, or even as a sandwich filling. Here it teams perfectly with chicken.

Serves 4

INGREDIENTS

juice of 2 lemons
45ml/3 tbsp olive oil
2 garlic cloves, crushed
5 chicken breast portions, 200g/7oz each
2 beefsteak tomatoes, cored and cut in half
salt and ground black pepper

For the avocado sauce

1 ripe avocado
50ml/2fl oz/¼ cup sour cream
45ml/3 tbsp fresh lemon juice
2.5ml/½ tsp salt
50ml/2fl oz/¼ cup water

To serve

chopped fresh coriander (cilantro), to garnish

1 Combine the lemon juice, oil, garlic, 2.5ml/½ tsp salt, and a little pepper in a bowl. Stir to mix.

2 Arrange the chicken portions in one layer in a shallow glass dish. Pour over the lemon mixture and turn to coat evenly. Cover and allow to stand for at least 1 hour at room temperature, or chill overnight.

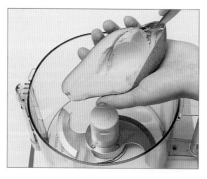

3 For the avocado sauce, cut the avocado in half, remove the stone (pit) and scrape the flesh into a food processor or blender.

4 Add the sour cream, lemon juice and salt, and process until smooth. Add the water and process just to blend. If necessary, add more water to thin the sauce. Transfer to a bowl, taste and adjust the seasoning, if necessary. Set aside.

5 Preheat the grill (broiler) to hot. Heat a ridged griddle or heavy frying pan. Remove the chicken from the marinade and pat dry.

6 When the griddle or frying pan is hot, add the chicken and cook, turning often, for about 10 minutes, until they are cooked through.

7 Meanwhile, arrange the tomato halves, cut-sides up, on a baking sheet and season lightly with salt and pepper. Grill (broil) for about 5 minutes, until hot and bubbling.

8 To serve, place a chicken portion, tomato half, and a spoonful of avocado sauce on each plate. Sprinkle with coriander and serve.

VARIATION

To cook the chicken on a barbecue, prepare the fire, and, when the coals are glowing red and covered with grey ash, spread them in a single layer. Set an oiled barbecue grill rack about 13cm/5in above the coals and cook the chicken portions for 15–20 minutes, until lightly charred and cooked through. Allow extra olive oil for basting.

Walnut and Pomegranate Sauce with Duck Breasts

THIS IS AN EXTREMELY EXOTIC sweet-and-sour sauce, which originally comes from Iran.

Serves 4

INGREDIENTS
4 duck breasts, about 225g/8oz each

For the walnut and pomegranate sauce
30ml/2 tbsp olive oil
2 onions, very thinly sliced
2.5ml/½ tsp ground turmeric
400g/14oz/2⅓ cups walnuts, roughly chopped
1 litre/1¾ pints/4 cups duck or chicken stock
6 pomegranates
30ml/2 tbsp caster (superfine) sugar
60ml/4 tbsp lemon juice
salt and ground black pepper

1 To make the sauce, heat half the oil in a frying pan. Add the onions and turmeric, and cook gently until soft.

2 Transfer to a pan, add the walnuts and stock, then season with salt and pepper. Stir, then bring to the boil and simmer the mixture, uncovered, for 20 minutes.

3 Cut the pomegranates in half and scoop out the seeds. Reserve the seeds of one pomegranate. Transfer the remaining seeds to a blender and process to break them up. Strain through a sieve, to extract the juice, and stir in the sugar and lemon juice.

4 Score the skin of the duck breasts in a diamond pattern with a sharp knife. Heat the remaining oil in a frying pan or griddle and place the duck breasts in it, skin-side down.

5 Cook gently for 10 minutes, pouring off the fat, until the skin is dark golden and crisp. Turn the duck over and cook for a further 3–4 minutes. Transfer to a plate and leave to rest. Deglaze the frying pan with the pomegranate juice, then add the walnut and stock mixture and simmer for 15 minutes until thickened.

6 Slice the duck and serve drizzled with a little sauce, and garnished with the reserved pomegranate seeds. Serve the remaining sauce separately.

Redcurrant Sauce with Lamb Burgers

THE SWEET-SOUR redcurrant sauce is the perfect complement to lamb and would go equally well with grilled or roast lamb steaks.

Serves 4

INGREDIENTS

500g/1¼lb minced (ground) lean lamb
1 small onion, finely chopped
30ml/2 tbsp finely chopped fresh mint
30ml/2 tbsp finely chopped fresh parsley
115g/4oz mozzarella cheese
30ml/2 tbsp oil, for basting
salt and ground black pepper

For the redcurrant sauce
115g/4oz/1 cup fresh or frozen redcurrants
10ml/2 tsp clear honey
5ml/1 tsp balsamic vinegar
30ml/2 tbsp finely chopped mint

1 In a large bowl, mix together the minced lamb, chopped onion, mint and parsley until evenly combined. Season well with plenty of salt and ground black pepper.

2 Roughly divide the meat mixture into eight equal pieces and use your hands to press each of the pieces into flat rounds.

3 Cut the mozzarella into four chunks. Place a chunk of cheese on half the lamb rounds. Top each with another round of meat mixture.

4 Press each of the two rounds of meat together firmly, making four flattish burger shapes. Use your fingers to blend the edges and seal in the cheese completely.

5 To make the sauce, place all the ingredients in a bowl and mash them together with a fork. Season well with salt and ground black pepper.

6 Brush the lamb burgers with olive oil and or grill (broil) for 10 minutes turning once, until golden brown. Serve with the sauce.

VARIATION

To make a quick version of the sauce, melt a jar of ready-made redcurrant sauce with balsamic vinegar and mint.

Tomato Sauce with Greek Lamb Sausages

FOR A QUICK AND EASY tomato sauce, passata can be enlivened with the addition of sugar, bay leaves and onions. The sausages will add more flavour as they simmer in the smooth sauce. As an alternative you could try using turkey instead of lamb.

Serves 4

INGREDIENTS

50g/2oz/1 cup fresh breadcrumbs
150ml/¼ pint/⅔ cup milk
675g/1½ lb minced (ground) lamb
30ml/2 tbsp grated onion
3 garlic cloves, crushed
10ml/2 tsp ground cumin
30ml/2 tbsp chopped fresh parsley
flour, for dusting
olive oil, for frying
salt and ground black pepper
fresh flat leaf parsley, to garnish

For the tomato sauce
600ml/1 pint/2½ cups passata (bottled strained tomatoes)
5ml/1 tsp sugar
2 bay leaves
1 small onion, peeled

1 Mix together the breadcrumbs and milk. Add the lamb, onion, garlic, cumin and parsley and season well.

2 Shape the mixture into little fat sausages, about 5cm/2in long and roll them in flour.

3 Heat about 60ml/4 tbsp olive oil in a pan. Fry the sausages in the oil for about 8 minutes, turning them until evenly browned. Remove and place on kitchen paper to drain.

4 Put the passata, sugar, bay leaves and whole onion in a pan and simmer for 20 minutes.

5 Add the sausages and cook for 10 minutes more. Serve garnished with parsley.

Pesto with Roast Leg of Lamb

THE INTENSE AROMAS OF fresh basil and garlic combine irresistibly with lamb, and the pine nuts and Parmesan make a delectable crunchy crust during roasting.

Serves 6

INGREDIENTS
2.25–2.75kg/5–6lb leg of lamb

For the pesto
90g/3½oz/1¾ cups fresh basil leaves
4 garlic cloves, coarsely chopped
45ml/3 tbsp pine nuts
150ml/¼ pint/⅔ cup olive oil
50g/2oz/⅔ cup freshly grated Parmesan cheese
5ml/1 tsp salt, or to taste

1 To make the pesto, combine the basil, garlic and pine nuts in a food processor, and process until finely chopped. With the motor running, slowly add the oil in a steady stream. Scrape the mixture into a bowl. Stir in the Parmesan and salt.

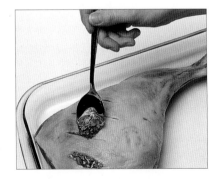

2 Set the lamb in an ovenproof dish. Make several slits in the meat with a knife, and spoon pesto into each slit.

3 Coat the surface of the lamb in a thick, even layer of the remaining pesto. Cover the meat and leave to stand for 2 hours at room temperature, or chill overnight. Preheat the oven to 180°C/350°F/Gas 4.

4 Place the lamb in the oven and roast, allowing about 20 minutes per 450g/1lb if you like rare meat, or 25 minutes per 450g/1lb if you prefer it medium-rare. Turn the lamb occasionally during roasting.

5 Remove the leg of lamb from the oven, cover it loosely with foil, and let it rest for about 15 minutes before carving and serving.

VARIATION

Lamb steaks or lamb chops could also be coated with this delicious pesto.

Sage and Orange Sauce with Pork Fillet

SAGE IS OFTEN PARTNERED with pork – there seems to be a natural affinity – and the addition of orange to the sauce balances the flavour.

Serves 4

INGREDIENTS

2 x 350g/12oz pork fillets (tenderloin)
10ml/2 tsp unsalted (sweet) butter
salt and ground black pepper
orange wedges and sage leaves, to garnish

For the sage and orange sauce
120ml/4fl oz/¹/₂ cup dry sherry
175ml/6fl oz/³/₄ cup chicken stock
2 garlic cloves, very finely chopped
grated rind and juice of 1 unwaxed orange
3–4 sage leaves, finely chopped
10ml/2 tsp cornflour (cornstarch)

1 Season the pork fillets lightly with salt and pepper.

2 Melt the butter in a heavy, flame-proof casserole over a medium-high heat, then add the meat and cook for 5 minutes, turning to brown all sides evenly.

3 Add the sherry, boil for about 1 minute, then add the stock, garlic, orange rind and chopped sage. Bring to the boil and reduce the heat to low, then cover and simmer for 20 minutes, turning once.

4 Transfer the pork to a warmed platter and cover to keep warm.

5 Bring the sauce to the boil. Blend the cornflour and orange juice and stir into the sauce, then boil gently over a medium heat for a few minutes, stirring frequently, until the sauce is slightly thickened.

6 Slice the pork diagonally and pour the meat juices into the sauce.

7 Spoon a little sauce over the pork and garnish with orange wedges and sage leaves. Serve the remaining sauce separately.

COOK'S TIP

• *The meat is cooked if the juices run clear when the meat is pierced, or when a meat thermometer inserted into the thickest part of the meat registers 66°C/150°F.*
• *If fresh sage is not available, try using rosemary as a substitute, as this also goes very well with pork.*

Cumberland Sauce with Gammon

THIS SAUCE WAS INVENTED to honour the Duke of Cumberland, who commanded the troops at the last battle on English soil, against the Scots. It can be served hot or cold, with gammon or venison.

Serves 8–10

INGREDIENTS

2.25kg/5lb smoked or unsmoked
  gammon (cured ham) joint
1 onion
1 carrot
1 celery stick
bouquet garni sachet
6 peppercorns

For the glaze
whole cloves
50g/2oz/¹⁄₄ cup soft light brown or
  demerara (raw) sugar
30ml/2 tbsp golden (light corn) syrup
5ml/1 tsp English (hot) mustard powder

For the Cumberland sauce
juice and shredded rind of 1 orange
30ml/2 tbsp lemon juice
120ml/4fl oz/¹⁄₂ cup port or red wine
60ml/4 tbsp redcurrant jelly

1 Soak the gammon overnight in a cool place in plenty of cold water to cover. Discard this water. Put the joint into a large pan and cover it again with more cold water. Bring the water to the boil slowly and skim any scum from the surface with a slotted spoon.

2 Add the vegetables and seasonings, cover and simmer very gently for 2 hours. (The meat can also be cooked in the oven at 180°C/350°F/ Gas 4. Allow 30 minutes per 450g/1lb.)

3 Leave the meat to cool in the liquid for 30 minutes. Then remove it from the liquid and strip off the skin neatly with the help of a knife (use rubber gloves if the gammon is too hot to handle).

4 Score the fat in diamonds with a sharp knife and stick a clove in the centre of each diamond. Preheat the oven to 180°C/350°F/Gas 4.

5 Put the sugar, syrup and mustard powder in a small pan and heat gently to melt them. Place the gammon in a roasting pan and spoon over the glaze. Bake it for about 20 minutes, or until golden brown, then put it under a hot grill (broiler) to colour.

6 Allow the meat to stand in a warm place for 15 minutes before carving (this makes carving much easier and tenderizes the meat).

7 For the Cumberland sauce, put the orange and lemon juice into a pan with the port or wine and redcurrant jelly, and heat gently to melt the jelly. Pour boiling water on to the orange rind, strain, and add the rind to the sauce. Cook gently for two minutes. Serve the sauce hot.

COOK'S TIP

Gammon is often not as strongly salted as it once was, so it may not be necessary to soak overnight before cooking to remove the salty flavour.

Black Bean Sauce with Beef and Broccoli Stir-fry

THIS CHINESE BEEF DISH is a quick stir-fry with a richly flavoured marinade that bubbles down into a luscious, dark sauce.

Serves 4

INGREDIENTS

225g/8oz lean fillet or rump (round) steak
15ml/1 tbsp sunflower oil
225g/8oz broccoli
115g/4oz baby corn, diagonally halved
45–60ml/3–4 tbsp water
2 leeks, diagonally sliced
225g/8oz can water chestnuts, sliced

For the marinade

15ml/1 tbsp fermented black beans
30ml/2 tbsp dark soy sauce
30ml/2 tbsp Chinese rice vinegar or
    (hard) cider vinegar
15ml/1 tbsp sunflower oil
5ml/1 tsp sugar
2 garlic cloves, crushed
2.5cm/1in piece of fresh root ginger, peeled
    and finely chopped

To make the marinade, mash the fermented black beans in a non-metallic bowl. Add the remaining ingredients and stir well.

2 Cut the steak into thin slices across the grain, then add them to the marinade. Stir the steak well to coat it in the marinade. Cover the bowl and leave for several hours.

3 Heat the oil in a frying pan. Drain the steak (reserving the marinade). When the oil is hot, add the meat and stir-fry for 3–4 minutes. Transfer to a plate and set aside.

4 Cut the broccoli into small florets. Reheat the oil in the pan, add the broccoli, corn and water. Cover and steam gently for 5 minutes.

5 Add the leeks and water chestnuts to the broccoli mixture and toss over the heat for 1–2 minutes. Return the meat to the pan, pour over the reserved marinade and toss briefly over a high heat before serving.

COOK'S TIP

Fermented black beans are cooked, salted and fermented whole soya beans; they are available from Asian stores.

Roquefort and Walnut Butter with Rump Steak

MAKE A ROLL OF this savoury cheese butter to keep in the refrigerator, ready to top plain steaks or chops.

Serves 4

INGREDIENTS

15ml/1 tbsp finely chopped fresh chives
15ml/1 tbsp olive oil or sunflower oil
4 x 130g/4½oz lean rump (round) steaks
120ml/4fl oz/½ cup dry white wine
30ml/2 tbsp crème fraîche
salt and ground black pepper
fresh chives, to garnish

For the Roquefort and walnut butter

2 shallots, chopped
75g/3oz/6 tbsp butter, slightly softened
150g/5oz Roquefort cheese
30ml/2 tbsp finely chopped walnuts

1 Sauté the shallots in one-third of the butter. Tip into a bowl and add half the remaining butter, the cheese, walnuts, chopped chives and pepper to taste. Chill lightly, roll in foil to a sausage shape and chill again until firm.

2 Heat the remaining butter with the oil and cook the steaks to your liking. Season and remove from the pan.

3 Pour the wine into the pan and stir to incorporate any sediment. Bubble up the liquid for a minute or two, then stir in the crème fraîche. Season with salt and pepper and pour over the steaks.

4 Cut pats of the Roquefort butter from the roll and put one on top of each steak. Garnish with chives and serve. Green beans make an ideal accompaniment to this dish.

COOK'S TIP

The butter can also be stored in the freezer, but it is easier to cut it into rounds before freezing, so you can remove just as many as you need, without thawing the rest.

Sauces for Fish Dishes

You might expect all sauces for fish to be very delicate and light in flavour, but that's not always the case. Certainly in this chapter you'll find a classic white parsley sauce: the perfect partner for white fish or fishcakes. But you'll also discover some more surprising combinations – a tangy orange butter sauce to pep up plain white fish, and a chilli barbecue sauce to serve with salmon steaks. As with any sauce, there are no hard-and-fast rules, but the general guideline is that white fish pairs best with subtle cream sauces and herb butters, whereas oily fish can take more robust flavours, such as spices or tangy fruits.

Parsley Sauce with Haddock

ONE OF THE MOST classic sauces for fish is parsley sauce – a perfect partner for any white fish.

Serves 4

INGREDIENTS

4 haddock fillets, about 175g/6oz each
25g/1oz/2 tbsp butter
150ml/¼ pint/⅔ cup milk
150ml/¼ pint/⅔ cup fish stock
1 bay leaf
salt and ground black pepper

For the parsley sauce

25g/1oz/2 tbsp butter
20ml/4 tsp plain (all-purpose) flour
60ml/4 tbsp single (light) cream
1 egg yolk
45ml/3 tbsp chopped fresh parsley
grated rind and juice of ½ lemon

1 Place the fish in a frying pan, add the butter, milk, fish stock, bay leaf and seasoning, and heat to simmering point.

2 Lower the heat, cover the pan and poach the fish for 10–15 minutes, depending on the thickness of the fillets, until the fish is tender and the flesh begins to flake. Transfer to a warm serving plate, cover and keep warm.

3 Make the sauce. Return the cooking liquid to the heat and bring to the boil, stirring. Simmer for about 4 minutes, then remove and discard the bay leaf.

4 Melt the butter in a pan, stir in the flour and cook, stirring constantly, for 1 minute.

5 Remove the pan from the heat and gradually stir in the fish cooking liquid.

6 Return to the heat and bring to the boil, stirring. Simmer for about 4 minutes, stirring frequently. Remove the pan from the heat.

7 In a bowl, blend the cream into the egg yolk, then stir this into the sauce with the parsley.

8 Reheat gently, stirring, for a few minutes; do not allow to boil.

9 Remove from the heat and add the lemon juice and rind, and season to taste. Pour into a warmed sauceboat and serve with the fish.

Vermouth and Chèvre Sauce with Pan-fried Cod

A SMOOTH SAUCE OF vermouth and light, creamy chèvre teams deliciously with chunky, white cod.

Serves 4

INGREDIENTS

4 cod fillets, about 150g/5oz each, skinned
15ml/1 tbsp olive oil
salt and ground black pepper
fresh flat leaf parsley, to garnish

For the vermouth and chèvre sauce
15ml/1 tbsp olive oil
4 spring onions (scallions), chopped
150ml/¼ pint/⅔ cup dry vermouth,
   preferably Noilly Prat
300ml/½ pint/1¼ cups fish stock
45ml/3 tbsp crème fraîche
65g/2½ oz chèvre (goat's cheese),
   rind removed, and chopped
30ml/2 tbsp chopped fresh parsley
15ml/1 tbsp chopped fresh chervil

Remove any stray bones from the cod fillets. Rinse the fish under cold running water and pat dry with kitchen paper. Place the pieces on a plate and season generously.

VARIATION

Instead of cod you could use salmon, haddock or plaice. The cooking time may change according to the thickness of the fish fillets.

2 Heat a non-stick frying pan, then add the oil, swirling it around to coat the base. Add the pieces of cod and cook, without turning or moving them, for 4 minutes, or until nicely caramelized.

3 Turn each piece over and cook the other side for a further 3 minutes, or until just firm. Remove them to a serving plate and keep hot.

4 To make the sauce, heat the oil in a frying pan and stir-fry the spring onions for 1 minute. Add the vermouth and cook until reduced by half. Add the stock and cook again until reduced by half. Stir in the crème fraîche and chèvre and simmer for about 3 minutes.

5 Add salt and pepper to taste, stir in the herbs and spoon over the fish. Garnish with parsley.

Five-spice and Black Bean Sauce with Stir-fried Squid

THE SPICY ASIAN SAUCE is the ideal accompaniment for stir-fried squid and is very easy to make. It is important to have all the ingredients ready before you start to cook. The squid must be cooked very quickly or it will toughen.

Serves 6

INGREDIENTS

450g/1lb small squid, cleaned
45ml/3 tbsp oil

For the five-spice and black bean sauce

2.5cm/1in piece fresh root ginger, grated
1 garlic clove, crushed
8 spring onions (scallions), cut diagonally
   into 2.5cm/1in lengths
1 red (bell) pepper, seeded and sliced
1 fresh green chilli, seeded and thinly sliced
6 chestnut mushrooms, sliced
5ml/1 tsp five-spice powder
30ml/2 tbsp black bean sauce
30ml/2 tbsp soy sauce
5ml/1 tsp sugar
15ml/1 tbsp rice wine or dry sherry

1 Rinse the squid and pull away the outer skin. Dry on kitchen paper. Slit the squid open and score the outside into diamonds with a sharp knife. Cut the squid into strips.

2 Heat a wok and add the oil. When it is hot, stir-fry the squid quickly. Remove the squid strips from the wok with a slotted spoon and set aside.

3 For the sauce, add the ginger, garlic, spring onions, red pepper, chilli and mushrooms to the oil remaining in the wok and stir-fry for 2 minutes.

4 Return the squid to the wok and stir in the five-spice powder. Stir in the black bean sauce, soy sauce, sugar and rice wine or sherry. Bring to the boil and cook, stirring, for 1 minute. Serve immediately.

Gooseberry Sauce with Mackerel

GOOSEBERRIES AND MACKEREL ARE a classic combination; the tart sauce offsets the rich, oily fish.

Serves 4

INGREDIENTS
4 fresh mackerel, about 350g/12oz
    each, cleaned
salt and ground black pepper

For the gooseberry sauce
15g/½oz/1 tbsp butter
225g/8oz gooseberries, trimmed
1 egg, beaten
pinch of ground mace or ginger, or a few
    drops of orange flower water (optional)
fresh flat leaf parsley, to garnish

1 Melt the butter in a pan, add the gooseberries, then cover and cook over a low heat, shaking the pan until the gooseberries are just tender.

2 Meanwhile, preheat the grill (broiler). Season the fish inside and out with salt and black pepper.

3 Cut two or three slashes in the skin on both sides of each mackerel, then grill (broil) for 15–20 minutes, or until cooked, turning once.

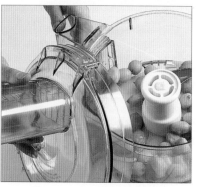

4 Purée the gooseberries with the egg in a food processor or blender, or mash the gooseberries thoroughly in a bowl with the egg. Press the gooseberry mixture through a sieve.

5 Return the gooseberry mixture to the pan and reheat gently, stirring, but do not allow to boil. Add the mace, ginger or orange flower water, if using, and season to taste. Serve the sauce hot with the mackerel, garnished with fresh parsley.

COOK'S TIPS

• For the best flavour, look for triple strength orange flower water, which can be obtained from chemists (drugstores) and good food stores.
• If fresh gooseberries are not in season, canned ones make an alternative. Make sure they do not contain added sugar or the tart flavour will not be achieved.

Herb Sauce with Sardines

THE ONLY ESSENTIAL ACCOMPANIMENT to this luscious herb sauce is fresh, crusty bread to mop up the tasty juices. The sauce is also quite delicious served with plain chicken breast portions. For the best flavour, cook the sardines on a barbecue.

Serves 4

INGREDIENTS

12–16 fresh sardines
oil, for brushing
juice of 1 lemon
crusty bread, to serve

For the herb sauce
15ml/1 tbsp butter
4 spring onions (scallions), chopped
1 garlic clove, finely chopped
grated rind of 1 lemon
30ml/2 tbsp finely chopped fresh parsley
30ml/2 tbsp finely chopped fresh chives
30ml/2 tbsp finely chopped fresh basil
30ml/2 tbsp green olive paste
10ml/2 tsp balsamic vinegar
salt and ground black pepper

3 Add the lemon rind and remaining sauce ingredients to the onions and garlic in the pan and keep warm on the edge of the hob (stovetop) or barbecue, stirring occasionally. Do not allow the mixture to boil.

4 Brush the sardines lightly with oil and sprinkle with lemon juice, salt and pepper. Cook on a barbecue (grill) for about 2 minutes on each side, over a medium heat. Serve with the warm sauce and fresh crusty bread.

1 To clean the sardines, use a pair of small kitchen scissors to slit the fish along the belly and pull out the innards. Wipe the fish with kitchen paper and then arrange on a wire rack.

2 To make the sauce, melt the butter in a small pan and gently sauté the spring onions and garlic for about 2 minutes, shaking the pan occasionally, until softened but not browned.

Orange Butter Sauce with Sea Bream

3 Place the orange juice concentrate in a bowl and heat over a pan of simmering water. Remove the pan from the heat and gradually whisk in the butter until creamy. Season well.

4 Dress the salad leaves with the remaining olive oil, and arrange with the fish on two plates. Spoon the sauce over the fish and serve.

THIS RICH BUTTER SAUCE, sharpened with tangy orange juice, goes well with the firm white flesh of sea bream.

Serves 2

INGREDIENTS

2 sea bream or porgy, about 350g/12oz
   each, scaled and gutted
10ml/2 tsp Dijon mustard
5ml/1 tsp fennel seeds
30ml/2 tbsp olive oil
225g/8oz mixed salad leaves

For the orange butter sauce

30ml/2 tbsp frozen orange
   juice concentrate
175g/6oz/¾ cup unsalted (sweet)
   butter, diced
salt and cayenne pepper

1 Slash the fish four times on each side. Combine the mustard and fennel seeds, then spread over both sides of the fish.

2 Brush each side of the fish with olive oil and grill (broil) under a preheated grill (broiler) for 10–12 minutes, turning the fish once midway through the cooking time.

COOK'S TIP

Alternatively, cook the fish on a medium-hot barbecue. This is much easier if you use a hinged wire rack that holds the fish firmly and enables you to turn the fish without it breaking up.

Tahini Sauce with Baked Fish

THIS NORTH AFRICAN RECIPE evokes all the colour and rich flavours of Mediterranean cuisine, and the tahini sauce makes an unusual combination of tastes.

Serves 4

INGREDIENTS

1 whole fish, about 1.2kg/2½ lb, scaled
    and cleaned
10ml/2 tsp coriander seeds
4 garlic cloves, sliced
10ml/2 tsp harissa sauce
90ml/6 tbsp olive oil
6 plum tomatoes, sliced
1 mild onion, sliced
3 preserved lemons or 1 fresh lemon
plenty of fresh herbs, such as bay leaves,
    thyme and rosemary
salt and ground black pepper
extra herbs, to garnish

For the tahini sauce

75ml/2½ fl oz/⅓ cup light tahini
juice of 1 lemon
1 garlic clove, crushed
45ml/3 tbsp finely chopped fresh parsley
    or coriander (cilantro)

1 Preheat the oven to 200°C/400°F/ Gas 6. Grease the base and sides of a large, shallow ovenproof dish.

2 Slash the fish diagonally on both sides with a sharp knife. Finely crush the coriander seeds and garlic with a mortar and pestle. Mix with the harissa sauce and about 60ml/4 tbsp of the olive oil.

3 Spread a little of the harissa, coriander and garlic paste inside the cavity of the fish. Spread the remainder over each side of the fish and set aside.

4 Sprinkle the tomatoes, onion and preserved or quartered fresh lemon into the dish. Sprinkle with the remaining oil, and season. Put the fish on top. Tuck plenty of herbs around it.

5 Bake the fish, uncovered, for about 25 minutes, or until it has turned opaque – test by piercing the thickest part with a knife.

6 Meanwhile, to make the sauce, put the tahini, lemon juice, garlic and parsley or coriander in a small pan with 120ml/4fl oz/½ cup cold water, and add a little salt and ground black pepper to season. Cook gently until smooth and heated through. Garnish the fish with the herbs, and serve the sauce separately.

COOK'S TIP

If you can't get a suitable large fish, use small whole fish such as red mullet, red snapper or even cod or haddock steaks. Reduce the cooking time slightly.

Sorrel Sauce with Salmon Steaks

THE SHARP FLAVOUR OF the sorrel sauce balances the richness of the fish. The young plant has the mildest flavour, so try to buy the herb in its spring season when it is at its best.

Serves 2

INGREDIENTS

2 salmon steaks, about 250g/9oz each
5ml/1 tsp olive oil
salt and ground black pepper
fresh sage, to garnish

For the sorrel sauce
15g/¹/₂oz/1 tbsp butter
2 shallots, finely chopped
45ml/3 tbsp crème fraîche
90g/3¹/₂oz fresh sorrel leaves, washed and patted dry

1 Season the salmon steaks with salt and pepper. Brush a non-stick frying pan with the oil.

2 Make the sauce. In a small pan, melt the butter over a medium heat. Add the shallots and fry for 3 minutes, stirring frequently, until just softened.

3 Add the crème fraîche and the sorrel leaves to the shallots and cook until the sorrel is completely wilted, stirring constantly.

4 Meanwhile, place the frying pan over a medium heat until hot. Add the salmon steaks and cook for about 5 minutes, turning once, until the flesh is opaque next to the bone. If you're not sure, pierce the flesh with the tip of a sharp knife; the fish should flake easily.

5 Arrange the salmon steaks on two warmed plates, garnish with sage and serve with the sorrel sauce.

COOK'S TIP

If preferred, cook the salmon steaks in the microwave for 4–5 minutes, in a tightly covered dish, or according to the manufacturer's guidelines.

VARIATION

If sorrel is not available, use finely chopped watercress instead.

Chilli Barbecue Sauce with Salmon

THIS SPICY TOMATO AND mustard sauce is delicious served with chargrilled salmon fillets, especially if you cook them on a barbecue.

Serves 4

INGREDIENTS

4 salmon fillets, about 175g/6oz

For the chilli barbecue sauce
10ml/2 tsp butter
1 small red onion, finely chopped
1 garlic clove, finely chopped
6 plum tomatoes, diced
45ml/3 tbsp tomato ketchup
30ml/2 tbsp Dijon mustard
30ml/2 tbsp dark brown sugar
15ml/1 tbsp clear honey
5ml/1 tsp ground cayenne pepper
15ml/1 tbsp ancho chilli powder
15ml/1 tbsp ground paprika
15ml/1 tbsp Worcestershire sauce

1 To make the barbecue sauce, melt the butter in a large, heavy pan and cook the chopped onion and garlic over a low heat until they are tender and translucent.

2 Stir in the tomatoes and simmer for 15 minutes, stirring occasionally (to break up the tomato pieces).

3 Add the remaining sauce ingredients and simmer for a further 20 minutes.

4 Process the mixture until smooth, in a food processor fitted with a metal blade. Leave to cool.

5 Brush the salmon with the sauce and chill for at least 2 hours. Barbecue (grill) or grill (broil) for about 2–3 minutes on each side, brushing on the sauce when necessary. Serve drizzled with the remaining sauce.

Dill and Mustard Sauce with Sole

THIS SAUCE WILL GIVE A TANGY, Scandinavian flavour that is perfect with fish. Sole is used here but the dill and mustard would combine with virtually any fish.

Serves 3–4

INGREDIENTS

3–4 lemon sole fillets
melted butter, for brushing
salt and ground black pepper
lemon slices and dill sprigs, to garnish

For the dill and mustard sauce
25g/1oz/2 tbsp butter
20g/¾oz/3 tbsp plain (all-purpose) flour
300ml/½ pint/1¼ cups hot fish stock
15ml/1 tbsp white wine vinegar
45ml/3 tbsp chopped fresh dill
15ml/1 tbsp wholegrain mustard
10ml/2 tsp sugar
2 egg yolks

1 Preheat the grill (broiler) to medium-high. Brush the fish with melted butter, season on both sides and cut two or three slashes in the flesh. Grill (broil) for 4 minutes, then transfer to a warmed place and keep warm while you make the sauce.

2 Melt the butter over a medium heat and stir in the flour. Cook for 1–2 minutes over a low heat, stirring constantly to remove any lumps.

3 Remove from the heat and gradually blend in the hot stock. Return to the heat, bring to the boil, stirring constantly, then simmer for 2–3 minutes.

VARIATION

A fennel and mustard sauce could also be made using chopped fennel leaves instead of the dill. Replace the wholegrain mustard with Dijon.

4 Remove the pan from the heat and beat in the white wine vinegar, dill, mustard and sugar.

5 Using a fork, beat the yolks in a small bowl and gradually add a small quantity of hot sauce. Return to the pan, whisking vigorously. Continue whisking over a very low heat for a further minute. Serve immediately with the grilled sole, garnished with lemon slices and dill sprigs.

Tartare Sauce with Crab Cakes

WHEN SERVING ANY FRIED fish, tartare sauce is the traditional accompaniment, but it is also delicious with vegetables. Maryland is renowned for its shellfish, and these little crab cakes hail from there.

Serves 4

INGREDIENTS

675g/1½lb fresh white crab meat
1 egg, beaten
30ml/2 tbsp mayonnaise
15ml/1 tbsp Worcestershire sauce
15ml/1 tbsp sherry
30ml/2 tbsp finely chopped fresh parsley
15ml/1 tbsp finely chopped fresh chives
45ml/3 tbsp olive oil
salt and ground black pepper

For the tartare sauce
1 egg yolk
15ml/1 tbsp white wine vinegar
30ml/2 tbsp Dijon-style mustard
250ml/8fl oz/1 cup vegetable oil
30ml/2 tbsp fresh lemon juice
45ml/3 tbsp finely chopped spring onions (scallions)
30ml/2 tbsp chopped drained capers
45ml/3 tbsp finely chopped sour dill pickles
45ml/3 tbsp finely chopped fresh parsley

1 Pick over the crab meat, removing any shell or cartilage. Keep the pieces of crab as large as possible.

2 In a bowl, combine the beaten egg with the mayonnaise, Worcestershire sauce, sherry and herbs. Season to taste. Gently fold in the crab meat.

3 Divide the mixture into eight portions and gently form each into an oval cake.

4 Place on a baking sheet between layers of greaseproof (waxed) paper and chill for at least 1 hour.

5 To make the sauce, in a bowl, beat the egg yolk with a wire whisk. Add the vinegar, mustard, and seasoning, and whisk for about 10 seconds. Whisk in the oil in a slow, steady stream.

6 Add the lemon juice, spring onions, capers, sour dill pickles and parsley and mix well. Check the seasoning. Cover and chill.

7 Preheat the grill (broiler). Brush the crab cakes with the olive oil. Place on an oiled baking sheet, in one layer. Grill (broil) 15cm/6in from the heat until golden brown, about 5 minutes on each side. Alternatively, fry the crab cakes over a medium heat for a few minutes on each side. Serve the crab cakes hot with the tartare sauce.

COOK'S TIPS

For easier handling and to make the crab meat go further, add 50g/2oz/1 cup fresh breadcrumbs and 1 more egg to the crab mixture. Divide the mixture into 12 cakes to serve six. Use dill instead of chives if you prefer.

Butter Sauce with Salmon Cakes

THE LEMONY BUTTER SAUCE keeps the salmon fishcakes deliciously moist; they make a real treat for supper or a leisurely breakfast at the weekend.

Makes 6

INGREDIENTS

225g/8oz tail piece of salmon, cooked
30ml/2 tbsp chopped fresh parsley
2 spring onions (scallions), chopped
225g/8oz/2⅔ cups firm mashed potato
1 egg, beaten
50g/2oz/1 cup fresh white breadcrumbs
butter and oil, for frying (optional)
salt and ground black pepper

For the butter sauce
75g/3oz/6 tbsp butter
grated rind and juice of ½ lemon

1 Remove all the skin and bones from the fish and mash or flake it well. Add the chopped parsley, onions and 5ml/ 1 tsp of the lemon rind (from the sauce ingredients) and season with salt and black pepper.

2 Gently work in the potato and then shape into six rounds.

3 Chill the fishcakes for 20 minutes to allow them to firm up. Coat each fishcake well in egg and then the breadcrumbs. Grill (broil) gently for 5 minutes each side, or until golden, or fry in butter and oil over a medium-hot heat.

4 To make the butter sauce, in a pan, melt the butter over a gentle heat, then whisk in the remaining lemon rind and the lemon juice, together with 15–30ml/1–2 tbsp cold water. Season with salt and ground black pepper to taste. Simmer the sauce for a few minutes and then serve immediately with the fishcakes.

VARIATION

If you like, use a lime instead of the half lemon for a change of flavour. This butter sauce is a quick and easy accompaniment to virtually any fish.

COOK'S TIP

Tail pieces of salmon fillet are usually a good buy and do not contain bones, but any cut of salmon can be used for this dish, so look out for any that are on special offer.

Warm Green Tartare Sauce with Scallops

A COLOURFUL SAUCE THAT'S good with all kinds of fish and shellfish, particularly fresh scallops, and it looks stunning over black pasta.

Serves 4

INGREDIENTS

350g/12oz black tagliatelle
12 large scallops
60ml/4 tbsp white wine
150ml/¼ pint/⅔ cup fish stock
lime wedges and parsley sprigs, to garnish

For the warm green tartare sauce
120ml/4fl oz/½ cup crème fraîche
10ml/2 tsp wholegrain mustard
2 garlic cloves, crushed
30–45ml/2–3 tbsp fresh lime juice
60ml/4 tbsp chopped fresh parsley
30ml/2 tbsp chopped chives
salt and ground black pepper

1 To make the tartare sauce, blend the crème fraîche, mustard, garlic, lime juice, parsley, chives and seasoning together in a food processor or blender.

2 Cook the pasta in a large pan of boiling, salted water according to the instructions on the packet until *al dente*. Drain thoroughly.

3 Meanwhile, slice the scallops in half, horizontally. Keep any corals whole.

4 Put the white wine and fish stock into a pan. Heat to simmering point. Add the scallops and cook very gently for 3–4 minutes (no longer or they will become tough).

5 Remove the scallops from the pan. Boil the wine and stock to reduce by about half and add the tartare sauce to the pan. Heat gently to warm the sauce.

6 Replace the scallops and cook for 1 minute. Spoon over the pasta. Garnish with lime wedges and parsley.

COOK'S TIPS

• *If you are removing the scallops from the shells yourself, remember to wash them first in plenty of cold water.*
• *If the scallops are frozen, thaw them before cooking, as they will probably have been glazed with water and will need to be drained well.*

VARIATIONS

• *This sauce could be made equally well with fresh mussels.*
• *Instead of serving over pasta, this sauce would go particularly well with fish, such as monkfish, which has a flavour reminiscent of lobster.*

Sauces for Vegetarian Dishes

Vegetables are one of the most versatile of all ingredients. They can provide hearty, cold-weather meals, such as Parsley Sauce and Baked Marrow, and the family favourite, Cheddar Cheese Sauce with Cauliflower. For a tasty summer dish, steam fresh vegetables, and serve them as a warm vegetable salad with peanut sauce. These sauces can also be used to add flavour and texture to freshly cooked pasta, such as the Green Vegetable Sauce or the Wild Mushroom Sauce with Polenta and Gorgonzola. Any of these sauces will enhance and complement a variety of dishes – whether the flavours are similar or contrasting – if you choose carefully.

Parsley Sauce and Baked Marrow

THIS IS A REALLY glorious way with a simple and modest vegetable. Try to find a small, firm and unblemished specimen for this recipe, as the flavour will be sweet, fresh and delicate. Young marrows do not need peeling.

Serves 4

INGREDIENTS

1 small young marrow (large zucchini), about 900g/2lb
30ml/2 tbsp olive oil
15g/½oz/1 tbsp butter
1 onion, chopped
15ml/1 tbsp plain (all-purpose) flour
300ml/½ pint/1¼ cups milk and single (light) cream, mixed
30ml/2 tbsp chopped fresh parsley
salt and ground black pepper

1 Preheat the oven to 180°C/350°F/ Gas 4. Cut the marrow into pieces measuring about 5 x 2.5cm/2 x 1in.

2 Heat the oil and butter in a flame-proof casserole and fry the onion over a gentle heat until very soft.

3 Add the marrow and sauté for 1–2 minutes and then stir in the flour. Cook for a few minutes.

4 Stir the milk and cream into the vegetable mixture.

5 Add the parsley and seasoning, and stir well.

6 Cover and cook in the oven for 30–35 minutes. If liked, uncover for the final five minutes of cooking to brown the top. Alternatively, serve the marrow in its rich, pale sauce.

VARIATION

Chopped fresh basil or a mixture of basil and chervil also tastes good in this dish.

Green Vegetable Sauce

THIS SAUCE IS A medley of cooked fresh vegetables. Tossed with pasta, it's ideal for a fresh, light lunch or supper dish.

Serves 4

INGREDIENTS
450g/1lb dried pasta shapes

For the green vegetable sauce
25g/1oz/2 tbsp butter
45ml/3 tbsp extra virgin olive oil
1 small leek, thinly sliced
2 carrots, diced
2.5ml/¹/₂ tsp sugar
1 courgette (zucchini), diced
75g/3oz/generous ¹/₂ cup green beans
115g/4oz/1 cup frozen peas
1 handful fresh flat leaf parsley, chopped
2 ripe plum tomatoes, peeled and diced
salt and ground black pepper
fried parsley sprigs, to garnish

1 Melt the butter and oil in a medium frying pan. When the mixture sizzles, add the prepared leek and carrots. Sprinkle the sugar over the vegetables and fry over a medium heat, stirring the mixture frequently, for about 5 minutes.

2 Stir the courgette, beans and peas into the sauce, and season with plenty of salt and pepper. Cover and cook over a low to medium heat for 5–8 minutes, or until the vegetables are tender, stirring occasionally.

3 Meanwhile, cook the pasta according to the instructions on the packet.

4 Stir the parsley and chopped tomatoes into the sauce.

5 Serve the sauce immediately, tossed with freshly cooked pasta and garnished with parsley sprigs.

Roasted Pepper Sauce with Malfatti

A SMOKY PEPPER AND tomato sauce adds the finishing touch to spinach and ricotta dumplings. The Italians call these malfatti – badly made – because of their odd shape.

Serves 4

INGREDIENTS

500g/1¼lb young leaf spinach
1 onion, finely chopped
1 garlic clove, crushed
15ml/1 tbsp extra virgin olive oil
350g/12 oz/1½ cups ricotta cheese
3 eggs, beaten
50g/2oz/scant 1 cup undyed
   dried breadcrumbs
50g/2oz/½ cup plain (all-purpose) flour
50g/2 oz/⅔ cup freshly grated
   Parmesan cheese
freshly grated nutmeg
25g/1oz/2 tbsp butter, melted

For the roasted pepper sauce

2 red (bell) peppers, seeded and quartered
30ml/2 tbsp extra virgin olive oil
1 onion, chopped
400g/14oz can chopped tomatoes
150ml/¼ pint/⅔ cup water
salt and ground black pepper

1 Make the sauce. Preheat the grill (broiler) and grill (broil) the pepper quarters skin-side up until they blister and blacken. Cool slightly, then peel off the skins and chop the flesh.

2 Heat the oil in a pan and lightly sauté the onion and peppers for 5 minutes.

3 Add the tomatoes and water, with salt and pepper to taste. Bring to the boil, lower the heat and simmer gently for 15 minutes.

4 Purée the mixture in a food processor or blender, in batches if necessary, then return to the clean pan and set aside.

5 Trim any thick stalks from the spinach, wash it well if necessary, then blanch in a pan of boiling water for about 1 minute. Drain, refresh under cold water and drain again. Squeeze dry, then chop finely.

6 Put the finely chopped onion, garlic, olive oil, ricotta, eggs and breadcrumbs in a bowl. Add the spinach and mix well. Stir in the flour and 5ml/1 tsp salt with half the Parmesan, then season to taste with pepper and nutmeg.

7 Roll the mixture into 16 small logs and chill lightly.

8 Bring a large pan of water to the boil. Drop in the malfatti in batches and cook them for 5 minutes. Remove with a fish slice (spatula) and toss with the melted butter.

9 To serve, reheat the sauce and divide it among four plates. Arrange four malfatti on each and sprinkle the remaining Parmesan over. Serve immediately.

Peanut Sauce with Warm Vegetable Salad

THIS SPICY SAUCE IS based on the classic Indonesian sauce served with satay, but is equally delicious served with this main-course salad which mixes steamed and raw vegetables. It would also partner vegetable kebabs cooked on a barbecue.

Serves 2–4

INGREDIENTS

8 new potatoes
225g/8oz broccoli, cut into small florets
200g/7oz/1⅓ cups fine green beans
2 carrots, cut into thin ribbons with a
  vegetable peeler
1 red (bell) pepper, seeded and sliced
50g/2oz sprouted beans
salad leaves, to garnish

For the peanut sauce
15ml/1 tbsp sunflower oil
1 bird's eye chilli, seeded and sliced
1 garlic clove, crushed
5ml/1 tsp ground coriander
5ml/1 tsp ground cumin
60ml/4 tbsp crunchy peanut butter
75ml/5 tbsp water
15ml/1 tbsp dark soy sauce
1cm/½in piece fresh root ginger,
  finely grated
5ml/1 tsp soft dark brown sugar
15ml/1 tbsp lime juice
60ml/4 tbsp coconut milk

First make the peanut sauce. Heat the oil in a pan, add the chilli and garlic, and cook for 1 minute, or until softened. Add the spices and cook for a further 1 minute.

2 Stir in the peanut butter and water, then cook for 2 minutes, or until combined, stirring constantly.

3 Add the soy sauce, ginger, sugar, lime juice and coconut milk, then cook over a low heat until smooth and heated through, stirring frequently. Transfer to a bowl.

4 Bring a pan of lightly salted water to the boil, add the potatoes and cook for 10–15 minutes, or until tender. Drain, then halve or thickly slice the potatoes, depending on their size.

5 Meanwhile, steam the broccoli and green beans for 4–5 minutes, or until tender but still crisp. Add the carrots 2 minutes before the end of the cooking time.

6 Arrange the cooked vegetables on a serving platter with the red pepper and sprouted beans. Garnish with salad leaves and serve with the peanut sauce.

COOK'S TIP

Adjust the dipping consistency by adding slightly less water than recommended; you can always stir in a little more at the last minute. Serve the sauce either warm or cold.

Quick Tomato Sauce with Baked Cheese Polenta

This quick tomato sauce can be prepared from pantry ingredients. The rich flavour of the sauce enhances baked polenta.

Serves 4

INGREDIENTS

5ml/1 tsp salt

250g/9oz/2¼ cups quick-cook polenta

5ml/1 tsp paprika

2.5ml/½ tsp ground nutmeg

75g/3oz/¾ cup grated Gruyère cheese

For the quick tomato sauce

30ml/2 tbsp olive oil

1 large onion, finely chopped

2 garlic cloves, crushed

2 x 400g/14oz cans chopped tomatoes

15ml/1 tbsp tomato purée (paste)

5ml/1 tsp sugar

salt and ground black pepper

1 Preheat the oven to 200°C/400°F/ Gas 6. Line a 28 x 18cm/11 x 7in baking tin (pan) with clear film (plastic wrap). Bring 1 litre/1¾ pints/4 cups water to the boil with the salt.

2 Pour in the quick-cook polenta in a steady stream and cook, stirring constantly, for 5 minutes. Beat in the paprika and nutmeg, then pour into the prepared tin and smooth the surface. Leave to cool.

3 To make the quick tomato sauce, heat the oil in a pan and cook the onion and garlic until soft. Add the chopped tomatoes, tomato purée and sugar. Season, and simmer for 20 minutes.

4 Turn out the polenta on to a board, and cut into 5cm/2in squares. Place half the squares in a greased ovenproof dish. Spoon over half the tomato sauce, and sprinkle with half the cheese. Repeat the layers. Bake for 25 minutes.

Fresh Tomato and Ginger Sauce with Tofu and Potato Rösti

IN THIS RECIPE, the tofu is marinated in a mixture of tamari, honey and oil, flavoured with garlic and ginger. This marinade is then added to the fresh tomatoes to make a thick, creamy tomato sauce with a delicious tang, and the method ensures that the tofu absorbs the same flavours.

Serves 4

INGREDIENTS

425g/15oz tofu, cut into 1cm/½in cubes
4 large potatoes, about 900g/2lb total
   weight, peeled
sunflower oil, for frying
salt and ground black pepper
30ml/2 tsp sesame seeds, toasted

For the fresh tomato and ginger sauce
30ml/2 tbsp tamari or dark soy sauce
15ml/1 tbsp clear honey
2 garlic cloves, crushed
4cm/1½in piece fresh root ginger, grated
5ml/1 tsp toasted sesame oil
15ml/1 tbsp olive oil
8 tomatoes, halved, seeded and chopped

1 For the sauce, mix together the tamari or dark soy sauce, clear honey, garlic, root ginger and toasted sesame oil in a shallow dish.

2 Add the tofu, then spoon the liquid over the tofu and leave to marinate in the refrigerator for at least 1 hour. Turn the tofu occasionally to allow the flavours to infuse (steep).

3 To make the rösti, par-boil the potatoes for 10–15 minutes until almost tender. Leave to cool, then grate coarsely. Season well with salt and freshly ground black pepper. Preheat the oven to 200°C/400°F/Gas 6.

4 Using a slotted spoon, remove the tofu from the marinade and reserve the marinade on one side. Spread out the tofu on a baking tray and bake for 20 minutes, turning occasionally, until golden and crisp on all sides.

5 Take one-quarter of the potato mixture in your hands at a time and form into rough cakes.

6 Heat a frying pan with just enough oil to cover the base. Place the cakes in the frying pan and flatten the mixture, using your hands or a spatula to form rounds about 1cm/½in thick.

7 Cook for about 6 minutes, or until golden and crisp underneath. Carefully turn the rösti over and cook for a further 6 minutes, or until golden brown in colour.

8 Meanwhile, complete the sauce. Heat the oil in a pan, add the reserved marinade and then the tomatoes and cook for 2 minutes, stirring constantly.

9 Reduce the heat and simmer, covered, for 10 minutes, stirring occasionally, until the tomatoes break down. Press the mixture through a sieve to make a thick, smooth sauce.

10 To serve, place a rösti on each of four warm serving plates. Arrange the tofu on top, spoon over the tomato sauce and sprinkle with sesame seeds.

COOK'S TIPS

• *Tamari is a thick, mellow-flavoured Japanese soy sauce, which is sold in Japanese food stores and some larger health-food stores.*
• *Tofu can be rather bland so allow it to marinate for 2–3 hours if possible, to ensure that it is full of flavour.*

Cheddar Cheese Sauce with Cauliflower

SELECT A MATURE FARMHOUSE Cheddar to give this popular dish a full flavour, and season with plenty of ground black pepper.

Serves 4

INGREDIENTS

1.2kg/2½ lb cauliflower florets
    (about 1 large head)
3 bay leaves

For the Cheddar cheese sauce
45ml/3 tbsp butter
45ml/3 tbsp plain (all-purpose) flour
450ml/¾ pint/scant 2 cups milk
50g/2oz/3 cups grated mature (sharp)
    Cheddar cheese
salt and ground black pepper

1 Preheat the oven to 180°C/350°F/ Gas 4. Grease a 30cm/12in round ovenproof dish.

2 Bring a large pan of lightly salted water to a boil. Add the cauliflower florets and cook for 7–8 minutes, or until just tender but still firm. Drain well.

3 To make the sauce, melt the butter in a heavy pan. Whisk in the flour until blended with the butter. Cook until smooth and bubbling, stirring constantly.

4 Gradually add the milk. Bring to a boil and continue cooking, stirring constantly, until the sauce is thickened and smooth.

5 Remove from the heat and stir in the cheese. Season the sauce to taste with salt and pepper.

6 Place the bay leaves on the bottom of the prepared dish. Arrange the cauliflower florets on top in an even layer. Pour the cheese sauce evenly over the cauliflower.

7 Bake for 20–25 minutes, or until golden brown and bubbling. Serve immediately.

VARIATION

You might like to try this with broccoli in place of cauliflower, or with a mixture of the two for a colourful change.

Wild Mushroom Sauce with Polenta and Gorgonzola

THE FLAVOUR OF WILD mushrooms combines well with mascarpone in this sauce to heighten the taste of the polenta. It also makes a delicious topping for baked potatoes.

Serves 4–6

INGREDIENTS

900ml/1½ pints/3¾ cups milk
900ml/1½ pints/3¾ cups water
5ml/1 tsp salt
300g/11oz/2¾ cups polenta
50g/2oz/¼ cup butter
115g/4oz Gorgonzola cheese
fresh thyme sprigs, to garnish

For the wild mushroom sauce
40g/1½ oz/scant 1 cup dried
  porcini mushrooms
150ml/¼ pint/⅔ cup hot water
25g/1oz/2 tbsp butter
115g/4oz/1½ cups button (white)
  mushrooms, chopped
60ml/4 tbsp dry white wine
generous pinch of dried thyme
60ml/4 tbsp mascarpone cheese
salt and ground black pepper

1 Pour the milk and water into a large, heavy pan. Add the salt and bring to the boil. Using a long-handled spoon, stir the liquid briskly with one hand while drizzling in the polenta with the other. When the mixture is thick and smooth, lower the heat to a gentle simmer and cook for about 20 minutes, stirring occasionally.

2 Remove from the heat and stir in the butter and Gorgonzola. Spoon the polenta mixture into a shallow dish and level the surface.

3 Let the polenta set until solid, then cut into wedges.

4 Meanwhile, make the sauce. Soak the porcini in the hot water for 15 minutes. Drain, reserving the liquid. Finely chop the porcini and strain the soaking liquid through a sieve lined with kitchen paper. Discard the kitchen paper.

5 Melt half the butter in a small pan. Sauté the chopped fresh mushrooms for about 5 minutes.

6 Add the wine, porcini and strained soaking liquid, with the dried thyme. Season to taste. Cook for 2 minutes more. Stir in the mascarpone and simmer for a few minutes, until reduced by one-third. Set aside to cool.

7 Heat a ridged griddle pan or grill (broiler), and cook the polenta until crisp. Brush with melted butter, garnish and serve hot with the sauce.

COOK'S TIP

If fresh porcini mushrooms are available, use instead of dried and do not soak. You will need about 175g/6oz fresh porcini for this recipe. They are also sold under the name ceps.

Sauces for Sweet Dishes

Hot and cold sweet sauces can transform a simple scoop of ice cream or a piece of fruit into a complete dessert. A good range of sweet sauces can increase your range of desserts three or four times over. Whether it's a tangy fruit coulis, a fragrant berry sauce or a simple hazelnut dip, you can mix and match your favourite desserts with sauces to create a new dish every time. Try a generous drizzle of chocolate sauce over profiteroles for a perfectly indulgent treat, or, for a lighter, less calorie-laden dish, how about maple yogurt sauce with poached pears or fresh strawberries.

Malted Chocolate and Banana Dip with Fresh Fruit

CHOCOLATE AND BANANA combine irresistibly in this rich dip, served with fresh fruit in season. For a creamier dip, stir in some lightly whipped cream just before serving.

Serves 4

INGREDIENTS

50g/2oz plain (semisweet) chocolate
2 large ripe bananas
15ml/1 tbsp malt extract (essence)
mixed fresh fruit, such as strawberries,
*   peaches and kiwi fruit, halved or sliced,*
*   to serve*

1 Break the chocolate into pieces and place in a small, heatproof bowl. Stand the bowl over a pan of gently simmering water and stir the chocolate occasionally until it melts. Allow to cool slightly.

2 Break the bananas into pieces and process in a food processor or blender until finely chopped.

3 With the motor running, pour in the malt extract, and continue processing the mixture until it is thick and frothy.

4 Drizzle in the chocolate in a steady stream and process until well blended. Serve immediately, with the prepared fruit alongside.

COOK'S TIP

This smooth dip can be prepared in advance and chilled.

Passion Fruit Coulis with Yogurt Sundaes

FROZEN YOGURT makes a refreshing change from ice cream. Here, it is partnered with a delicious fresh fruit coulis that is simple to make. Some varieties of strawberry may need a little sugar to sweeten them.

Serves 4

INGREDIENTS

175g/6oz/1½ cups strawberries, hulled and halved

2 peaches, stoned (pitted) and chopped

8 scoops (about 350g/12 oz) vanilla or strawberry frozen yogurt

For the passion fruit coulis

175g/6oz/1½ cups strawberries, hulled and halved

1 passion fruit

10ml/2 tsp icing (confectioners') sugar (optional)

1 To make the coulis, purée the strawberries. Scoop out the passion fruit pulp and add it to the coulis. Sweeten with icing sugar if necessary.

2 Spoon half the remaining strawberries and half the chopped peaches into four tall sundae glasses.

3 Add a scoop of frozen yogurt. Set aside a few choice pieces of fruit for decoration, and use the rest to make a further layer on the top of each sundae. Top each with a final scoop of frozen yogurt.

4 Pour the passion fruit coulis over, and decorate the sundaes with the reserved strawberries and pieces of peach. Serve immediately.

Hazelnut Dip with Fruit Fondue

FRESH FRUIT IS ALWAYS a good choice for a colourful, simple dessert, and this recipe makes it complete, with a delicious sauce for dipping. Any fruit which can be served raw can be used for this dish. Try to use fruits in a range of different colours for an attractive presentation.

Serves 2

INGREDIENTS

selection of fresh fruits, such as satsumas, kiwi fruit, grapes, physalis and whole strawberries

For the hazelnut dip

50g/2oz/¼ cup soft (farmer's) cheese

150ml/¼ pint/⅔ cup hazelnut yogurt

5ml/1 tsp vanilla essence (extract)

5ml/1 tsp caster (superfine) sugar

50g/2oz/⅓ cup shelled hazelnuts, chopped

1 First prepare the fruits. Peel and segment the satsumas. Then peel the kiwi fruit and cut into wedges. Wash the grapes and peel back the papery casing on the physalis.

2 To make the dip, beat the soft cheese with the hazelnut yogurt, vanilla essence and sugar in a bowl. Stir in three-quarters of the hazelnuts.

3 Spoon into a glass serving dish set on a platter or into small pots on individual plates and sprinkle the remaining hazelnuts on top. Arrange the prepared fruits around the dip and serve immediately.

Berry Sauce with Baked Ricotta Cakes

THE FLAVOUR OF THIS fragrant fruity sauce contrasts well with these honey and vanilla-flavoured desserts.

Serves 4

INGREDIENTS
250g/9oz/generous 1 cup ricotta cheese
2 egg whites, beaten
about 60ml/4 tbsp clear honey
few drops of vanilla essence (extract)
fresh mint leaves, to decorate (optional)

For the red berry sauce
450g/1lb/4 cups mixed fresh or frozen fruit, such as strawberries, raspberries, blackberries and cherries

COOK'S TIPS

• *The sauce can be made a day ahead. Chill until ready to use.*
• *Frozen fruit doesn't need extra water, as there will be ice crystals clinging to the berries.*

Preheat the oven to 180°C/350°F/ Gas 4.

2 Place the ricotta cheese in a bowl and break it up with a wooden spoon. Add the beaten egg whites, honey and vanilla essence and mix thoroughly until the mixture is smooth and well combined.

3 Lightly grease four ramekins. Spoon the ricotta mixture into the prepared ramekins and level the tops. Bake for 20 minutes or until the ricotta cakes are risen and golden.

4 Meanwhile, make the berry sauce. Reserve about one-quarter of the fruit for decoration. Place the rest of the fruit in a pan, with a little water if using fresh fruit, and heat gently until softened. Leave to cool slightly. Remove any cherry pits, if using.

5 Press the fruit through a sieve, then taste and sweeten with honey if it is too tart. Serve the sauce, warm or cold, with the ricotta cakes. Decorate with the reserved berries and mint leaves, if using.

Toffee Sauce with Hot Date Puddings

THIS TOFFEE SAUCE IS a great standby for hot or cold desserts. It is equally delicious served with poached apples or drizzled over a steamed pudding.

Serves 6

INGREDIENTS

50g/2oz/¼ cup butter, softened
75g/3oz/6 tbsp light muscovado
   (brown) sugar
2 eggs, beaten
115g/4oz/1 cup self-raising (self-rising) flour
2.5ml/½ tsp bicarbonate of soda
   (baking soda)
175g/6oz/generous 1 cup fresh dates,
   peeled, stoned (pitted) and chopped
75ml/5 tbsp boiling water
10ml/2 tsp coffee and chicory essence

For the toffee sauce

75g/3oz/6 tbsp light muscovado
   (brown) sugar
50g/2oz/¼ cup butter
60ml/4 tbsp double (heavy) cream
30ml/2 tbsp brandy

1 Preheat the oven to 180°C/350°F/ Gas 4. Place a baking sheet in the oven. Grease six pudding moulds.

2 Cream the butter and sugar in a large mixing bowl until pale and fluffy. Gradually add the beaten eggs a little at a time, beating well after each addition.

3 Sift the flour and bicarbonate of soda together and fold into the creamed mixture.

4 Put the dates in a heatproof bowl, pour over the boiling water and mash with a potato masher. Add the coffee and chicory essence, then stir the paste into the creamed mixture.

COOK'S TIP

It is preferable to peel the dates as the skins can be rather tough: simply squeeze them between your thumb and forefinger and the skins will pop off.

5 Spoon the mixture into the prepared moulds. Place on the hot baking sheet and bake for 20 minutes.

6 To make the toffee sauce, put all the ingredients in a pan and heat gently, stirring until smooth.

7 Increase the heat and boil for 1 minute. Turn the warm puddings out on to individual dessert plates. Spoon a generous amount of sauce over each and serve immediately.

Chocolate Sauce with Profiteroles

A REAL TREAT IF you're not counting calories, this sauce is also good with scoops of vanilla ice cream.

Serves 6

INGREDIENTS

65g/2½oz/9 tbsp plain (all-purpose) flour
50g/2oz/¼ cup butter
150ml/¼ pint/⅔ cup water
2 eggs, lightly beaten
150ml/¼ pint/⅔ cup whipping
   cream, whipped

For the chocolate sauce
150ml/¼ pint/⅔ cup double (heavy) cream
50g/2oz/¼ cup butter
50g/2oz/¼ cup vanilla sugar
175g/6oz plain (semisweet) chocolate
30ml/2 tbsp brandy

VARIATION

White chocolate and orange sauce
40g/1½oz/3 tbsp caster (superfine) sugar,
   to replace vanilla sugar
finely grated rind of 1 orange
175g/6oz white chocolate, to replace
   plain (semisweet) chocolate
30ml/2 tbsp orange liqueur, to
   replace brandy

1 Make the chocolate sauce. Heat the cream with the butter and vanilla sugar in a bowl over a pan of hot, but not boiling water. Stir until smooth, then cool.

2 Break the chocolate into the cream. Stir until it is melted and thoroughly combined.

3 Stir in the brandy a little at a time, then leave the sauce to cool to room temperature.

4 For the white chocolate and orange sauce, heat the cream and butter with the caster sugar and orange rind in the top of a double boiler, until dissolved. Use the white chocolate instead of plain chocolate in step 2, and orange liqueur instead of the brandy in step 3.

5 To make the profiteroles, preheat the oven to 200°C/400°F/Gas 6. Sift the flour on to a plate. Melt the butter and water in a pan and bring to the boil.

6 Remove the pan from the heat and tip the flour in all at once. Beat with a wooden spoon until smooth. Cool for 1–2 minutes, then gradually beat in enough egg to give a piping consistency. Beat well until glossy. Pipe small balls of the mixture on to dampened baking sheets.

7 Bake in the oven for 15–20 minutes, or until crisp. Make a slit in the sides and cool on a wire rack.

8 Fill a piping (pastry) bag with cream and pipe some into each profiterole. Pile on to a plate, topped with a little sauce. Serve the remaining chocolate sauce separately.

Papaya Sauce with Grilled Pineapple

TRY THE PAPAYA SAUCE with savoury dishes, too. It tastes great with grilled chicken and game birds as well as pork and lamb.

Serves 6

INGREDIENTS

1 sweet pineapple
melted butter, for greasing and brushing
2 pieces drained stem (crystallized) ginger in syrup, cut into fine matchsticks, plus 30ml/2 tsp syrup
30ml/2 tbsp demerara (raw) sugar
pinch of ground cinnamon
fresh mint sprigs, to decorate

For the papaya sauce
1 ripe papaya, peeled and seeded
175ml/6fl oz/¾ cup apple juice

1 Peel the pineapple and take spiral slices off the outside to remove the eyes. Cut it crossways into six slices, each 2.5cm/1in thick.

2 Line a baking sheet with a sheet of foil, rolling up the sides to make a rim. Grease the foil with melted butter. Preheat the grill (broiler).

VARIATION

If you like, substitute half apple juice and half papaya nectar for the apple juice in the sauce.

3 Arrange the pineapple slices on the baking sheet. Brush with butter, then top with ginger, sugar and cinnamon. Drizzle over the ginger syrup. Grill (broil) for 5–7 minutes, until the slices are lightly charred.

4 Cut a few slices from the papaya and set aside, then purée the rest together with the apple juice in a food processor or blender.

5 Press the purée through a sieve placed over a bowl, then stir in any juices from cooking the pineapple.

6 Serve the pineapple slices with a little sauce drizzled around each plate. Decorate with the reserved papaya slices and the mint sprigs.

Maple Yogurt Sauce with Poached Pears

THE SWEET-SOUR TASTE OF the maple syrup and yogurt will partner most poached fruit but is especially good with pears. Choose a firm but ripe pear such as Conference.

Serves 4

INGREDIENTS

4 firm dessert pears
15ml/1 tbsp lemon juice
250ml/8fl oz/1 cup sweet white wine
thinly pared rind of 1 lemon
1 cinnamon stick

For the maple yogurt sauce
pear cooking liquid
30ml/2 tbsp maple syrup
2.5ml/½ tsp arrowroot
150g/5oz/⅔ cup Greek (US strained
   plain) yogurt

1 Thinly peel the pears, leaving them whole and with stalks. Brush them with lemon juice, to prevent them from browning. Use a potato peeler or small knife to scoop out the core from the base of each pear.

2 Place the pears in a wide, heavy pan and pour the wine over them, with enough cold water almost to cover the pears.

3 Add the lemon rind and cinnamon stick and bring to the boil. Reduce the heat, cover the pan and simmer gently for 30–40 minutes, or until the pears are tender. Turn the pears occasionally so that they cook evenly. Lift them out carefully, draining them.

4 To make the sauce, bring the liquid to the boil and boil uncovered to reduce it to about 105ml/7 tbsp. Strain and add the maple syrup. Blend a little with the arrowroot. Return to the pan and cook, stirring, until thick. Cool.

5 Slice each cored pear about three-quarters of the way through, leaving the slices attached at the stem end. Fan out on a serving plate.

6 Stir 30ml/2 tbsp of the cooled syrup into the yogurt and spoon it around the pears. Drizzle with the remaining syrup and serve immediately.

VARIATION

If you want to make this sauce for another dessert, substitute fruit juice for the pear cooking liquid in step 4.

Strawberry Sauce with Lemon Hearts

THIS SPEEDY SWEET SAUCE makes a delicious accompaniment for these delicate lemon and cheese hearts.

Serves 4

INGREDIENTS

175g/6oz/¾ cup ricotta cheese
150ml/¼ pint/⅔ cup natural (plain) yogurt
15ml/1 tbsp sugar
finely grated rind of ½ lemon
30ml/2 tbsp lemon juice
10ml/2 tsp powdered gelatine
2 egg whites
oil, for greasing

For the strawberry sauce
225g/8oz/2 cups fresh or frozen and
    thawed strawberries, plus extra
    to decorate
15ml/1 tbsp lemon juice

1 Beat the ricotta until smooth. Stir in the yogurt, sugar and lemon rind.

2 Place the lemon juice in a small bowl and sprinkle the gelatine over it. Place the bowl over a pan of hot water and stir the mixture to dissolve the gelatine completely.

3 Beat the egg whites until they form soft peaks. Quickly stir the gelatine into the ricotta cheese mixture, mixing it in evenly, then immediately fold in the beaten egg whites.

4 Spoon the mixture into four lightly oiled, individual heart-shaped moulds and chill the moulds until set.

5 To make the sauce, place the strawberries and lemon juice in a food processor and process until smooth. Pour on to plates and top with turned-out hearts. Decorate with the extra strawberries.

VARIATION

Add a dash of Cointreau or Grand Marnier liqueur to the strawberry sauce.

Index